# Lights that Shine

**THE RESOURCE ROOM
CHURCH HOUSE
9 THE CLOSE
WINCHESTER
SO23 9LS**

# Lights that Shine

## How Christians can fulfil their call to mission

Shelagh Brown and Gavin Reid

Illustrations by Taffy

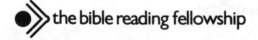
the bible reading fellowship

The Bible Reading Fellowship
Warwick House
25 Buckingham Palace Road
London SW1W OPP

First published 1991
© Shelagh Brown and Gavin Reid 1991

British Library Cataloguing in Publication Data

Reid, Gavin
    Lights that shine: how Christians can fulfil their
    call to mission.
    1. Christian church. Evangelism
    I. Title    II. Brown, Shelagh    III. Bible Reading Fellowship
    269.2

ISBN 0-900164-91-3


Typeset by Cambridge Composing (UK) Ltd
Printed by Bocardo Press Ltd, Didcot, England.

# Contents

# *Foreword*

by The Rt Revd Dr George Carey

The most urgent task the church has is that of sharing its faith with the world around. Look around at society's disintegrating morality, its ignorance of God, the apathy of many Christians and their failure to relate their faith to life – and you and I will need little convincing that the '90s will be a make-or-break decade.

I have, however, two grounds for my confidence that by the end of this decade the church will be a stronger and larger body.

The first is the power and presence of God. He has not given up believing in the world and in the church, and neither should we. Indeed, his grace and love are daily with us. We can trust in his power to equip his people for the work.

Secondly, we do have resources in the church to inform, challenge and inspire. An example is this splendid volume by Gavin Reid and Shelagh Brown. Written in a popular, light-hearted vein, the book is accessible to a wide variety of people without talking down to any of them.

So it gives me great pleasure to commend *Lights that Shine*; and I hope that it will assist us all to be relaxed and lively Christians who are ready to give an answer for the hope that is within us.

George Carey

# Introduction

When we were talking about what to call this book we wondered whether to have the word 'evangelism' in the title. After all, we were writing it for the Decade of Evangelism. But we thought that if we asked, 'Would you like to be an evangelist?', some people might be rather alarmed and say, 'No!'

A better question to ask seemed to be, 'Would you like to be lights that shine?' In answer to that we thought most people might smile a little, and say, 'Oh, yes!' So we have simply called it *Lights that Shine*, because that is what it is about.

It is Jesus who is the Light of the World. But in the Sermon on the Mount he says to his disciples:

You are the light of the world. A city on a hill cannot be hidden. **Matthew 5:14–16 NIV**
Neither do people light a lamp and put it under a bowl. Instead they put it on its stand, and it gives light to everyone in the house. In the same way, let your light shine before men, that they may see your good deeds and praise your Father in heaven.

ix

So here are six chapters all about how to let the light shine in the darkness of the world that God loves. We have written *Brushing up on Believing* to partner this book, because we are certain that the more deeply we believe the more brightly our lights will shine.

We have both been fully involved in writing both books. We met together over several months, either in the evenings or on Saturdays, and recorded long discussions on cassette. I (Shelagh) word-processed them, wrote the second drafts, and then we worked those over before I produced the final manuscript. But I have written them in the first person because they read better that way.

We now have considerable sympathy for Archbishop Derek Worlock and Bishop David Sheppard, who do various things together including writing books (one of them, *With Christ in the Wilderness*, for the Bible Reading Fellowship). It may be 'Better Together' (the title of one of their previous books) — and we believe that it is. But it is also a lot harder!

At the end of each chapter in this book we have included material for discussion (or consideration, if this is simply being read by individuals) together with prayers and meditations. Some readers will be experienced at leading groups, so they may make only a limited use of the material we have provided. But we had in mind the people who are less experienced, or perhaps have never led a group before, and we hope that the way we have set out the material will provide them with all they need.

Some readers will already know Graham Kendrick's song, 'Shine, Jesus, Shine'. Quite unusually, because of the importance of the Decade of Evangelism, Kingsway publications have given us permission to print the words and the music. We are thankful to them for the permission, to Graham Kendrick for writing it, and to the Holy Spirit for inspiring it. It would be a superb theme song for the Decade. It recognizes that the light of Christ is already shining in the world, but it is a prayer that it will shine even more brightly — both in the world and in our own hearts.

SHELAGH BROWN AND GAVIN REID

# Shine, Jesus, Shine

Capo 2(G)

Graham Kendrick

2. Lord, I come to Your awesome presence,
   From the shadows into Your radiance;
   By the blood I may enter Your brightness,
   Search me, try me, consume all my darkness.
   Shine on me, shine on me.

3. As we gaze on Your kingly brightness
   So our faces display Your likeness,
   Ever changing from glory to glory,
   Mirrored here may our lives tell Your story.
   Shine on me, shine on me.

   *(Chorus twice to end.)*

# 1. Where the Shining Starts

A seven-year-old girl was standing on the seashore at Blackpool listening with deep attention to the Salvation Army band. They were playing a song she had never heard before: 'I will make you fishers of men if you follow me . . .'

Jesus had spoken those words two thousand years ago, when he walked along the shore of Lake Galilee and called Simon and his brother Andrew to be his disciples. She didn't know that at the time. But she did know who was speaking, and it seemed to be to her.

In a way she said 'Yes'. Yet she didn't really have much option and she didn't want one. The one who spoke to her and the offer he made were irresistible and entirely satisfying. She wanted him, and she wanted to do what he said. But it has taken her most of her lifetime to discover what he meant.

I know a lot about her journey of discovery, because that seven-year-old on the seashore was me. I have taken a long time to put away childish things and become an adult in the area of evangelism. I thought too much about the fishing and not nearly enough about the following – so I failed to make the right connection between the two.

The children's chorus that spoke to my heart actually reverses the order of Jesus' words. The promise comes after the call: 'Follow me, and I will make you fishers of men.'

As the followers of Jesus, one of the things that we do is to cast out our nets and to catch fish, and this book is about the different ways of fishing. But often the 'fish' we have caught (and it is quite difficult to tell if we have succeeded or not) has only begun to follow – and the journey can start very slowly. Only sometimes do we see a fish landed neatly at our feet.

My own slowness to learn meant that I thought it always happened like that, always with clear divisions for me to see

2

between the fish who had been caught and the fish who hadn't: the person who was following Jesus and the person who wasn't. I don't know why I have been so dull in understanding, and my only comfort is that even Jesus' first disciples themselves were slow learners.

I know now that the parables and metaphors which Jesus used must not be pushed too far and that they usually have one main point. The point of this one is that those who are called to follow Jesus will be used by him, as we walk with him along the way, to capture the hearts of men and women for God in the power of the Spirit.

There are other biblical images to show us what it is like when a human being starts to know God. The Book of Proverbs says that it is like the light of dawn breaking slowly in the darkness. Sometimes I have looked out of my bedroom window in the early hours of a summer morning. From the east there is a faint shining – almost imperceptible. Then, slowly, it gets brighter, until the whole sky is full of light. That is how it is when the light of God starts to dawn in our hearts: 'The path of the righteous is like the first gleam of dawn, shining ever brighter till the full light of day' (Proverbs 4:18 NIV).

Matthew's gospel quotes the prophecy of Isaiah 9:2:

> The people living in darkness
>     have seen a great light;
> on those living in the land of the
>     shadow of death,
> a light has dawned.

**Matthew 4:16**
NIV

From that time on Jesus began to preach, 'Repent, for the kingdom of heaven is near.'

As Jesus was walking beside the Sea of Galilee, he saw two brothers, Simon called Peter and his brother Andrew. They were casting a net into the lake, for they were fishermen. 'Come, follow me,' Jesus said,

**Matthew**
4:18–20 NIV

'and I will make you fishers of men.' At once they left their nets and followed him.

The first thing that Jesus ever calls us to do is to follow him.

Everything else follows from that.

Gavin is very much involved nationally with the Decade of Evangelism, and it is increasingly being recognized that the first thing which has to be done is to help church people to become witnesses and affirmers of their faith. There is a task of teaching and training to be done, so that we don't feel at all ashamed of the gospel. Instead, we realize that we have a gospel that we can be proud about. Then we have to learn how to put in our own, faltering word of testimony when other people ask us about it.

When I run courses on the Christian faith I sometimes start by asking everyone to say why they have come and what they hope that they will get out of it. The answer that every person gives is almost always the same: 'I want to know God better, and I want to be able to share my faith.'

That answer gets the order right, and the double desire that struggles in people's hearts to be satisfied knows what comes first and what comes next. We have to know God for ourself before we can tell other people about him.

Some of us know him a little bit, and have a desire deep down in our heart to know him better. God has created us to know him and to love him and nothing else and no one else will ever satisfy us. The often-quoted words of St Augustine put it beautifully and perfectly: 'You have made us for Yourself, and our hearts are restless till they find their rest in You.'

The next thing I do in the courses I run is to ask everyone to tell the others, in just one sentence, how they think of God in their own hearts. If they want to they can refuse, and just say 'Pass'. But hardly anyone refuses, and that first, simple testimony, when one person tells other people about God, perhaps for the first time in their life, can be a seed that starts to grow.

After we had done that in one group a woman came back the next week with shining eyes. Someone had asked her about her own belief in God, and she had told them. She had never done it before, and she was exhilarated. The first letter of Peter says: 'Always be prepared to give an answer to everyone who asks you to give the reason for the hope that you have' (1 Peter 3:15 NIV).

We don't have to go rushing in. We can wait to be asked – and it is better to wait. But when we are asked then we must be able to give an answer, just as that woman did. All it has to be is a personal word of testimony – what the New Testament calls being a witness to Christ. Jesus told his disciples that what they had to do was to witness to him, and he promised them that he would give them the power to do it:

You will receive power when the Holy Spirit comes on you; and you **Acts 1:8 NIV** will be my witnesses in Jerusalem and in all Judaea, and Samaria, and to the ends of the earth.

Those first disciples told other people about Jesus. They went all over the known world and told them. They told them about his life and his death and his resurrection. They told them about the forgiveness of sins. And they told them that they knew in experience and by faith that Christ lived in their own hearts through the Holy Spirit. They knew Christ in a far deeper way than they had ever known him as a man – because now God-in-Christ was within them. The promise of how it was going to be is in the gospel (or the 'good news') according to John:

John 14:23 RSV If a man loves me, he will keep my word, and my Father will love him, and we will come to him and make our home with him.

Some of them had seen and known Jesus in the flesh. But they still had fellowship with him now – and that word 'fellowship' (Greek *koinonia*) means 'sharing'. They shared the same life as him, and it was the life of God. They also shared in that same life with all other Christians, because that is what it means to be a Christian.

God wants every human creature he has made to share in that life, and as Christians we want the same thing. At the start of his first letter John witnesses to what he and his fellow Christians knew of Christ and sets out the Christian message:

1 John 1:1–10 NIV That which was from the beginning, which we have heard, which we have seen with our eyes, which we have looked at and our hands have touched – this we proclaim concerning the Word of life. The life appeared; we have seen it and testify to it, and we proclaim to you the eternal life, which was with the Father and has appeared to us. We proclaim to you what we have seen and heard, so that you also may have fellowship with us. And our fellowship is with the Father and with his Son, Jesus Christ. We write this to make our joy complete.

This is the message we have heard from him and declare to you. God is light; in him there is no darkness at all. If we claim to have fellowship with him yet walk in the darkness, we lie and do not live by the truth. But if we walk in the light, as he is in the light, we have fellowship with one another, and the blood of Jesus, his Son, purifies us from all sin.

If we claim to be without sin, we deceive ourselves and the truth is not in us. If we confess our sins, he is faithful and just and will forgive us our sins and purify us from all unrighteousness. If we claim we have not sinned, we make him out to be a liar and his word has no place in our lives.

In the gospel of John Jesus appears to the disciples after his resurrection and sends them into the world to tell people about the forgiveness of sins:

On the evening of the first day of the week, when the disciples were together, with the doors locked for fear of the Jews, Jesus came and stood among them and said, 'Peace be with you!' After he said this, he showed them his hands and side. The disciples were overjoyed when they saw the Lord.

Again Jesus said, 'Peace be with you! As the Father has sent me, I am sending you.' And with that he breathed on them and said, 'Receive the Holy Spirit. If you forgive anyone his sins, they are forgiven; if you do not forgive them, they are not forgiven.'

John 20:19–23 NIV

It was not that the disciples were to forgive people's sins or not forgive them according to their own private whim, so that if they liked a person they would forgive her and if they didn't they wouldn't.

The forgiveness of sins happens because of what Christ has done. That is what the disciples made known in their preaching of the gospel as they journeyed all round the known world:

We have come here to tell you the good news that the promise made to our ancestors has come about. God has fulfilled it to their children by raising Jesus from the dead . . . My brothers, I want you to realise that it is through him that forgiveness of sins is being proclaimed to you. Through him justification from all sins from which the Law of Moses was unable to justify is being offered to every believer.

Acts 13:32–33; 38–39 NJB

If a man or a woman believed what they said and accepted the offer of forgiveness then the disciples (and those who preached the gospel after them) declared to them that their sins were forgiven and not retained. The belief and the acceptance of the offer included repentance, and that means to turn away from sin and to walk with Christ in the totally opposite way and into a new life.

In the account of the Day of Pentecost in the book of Acts we are told how the Holy Spirit came to all the disciples and how the apostle Peter then preached to a vast crowd of people about Jesus and the resurrection and the forgiveness of sins.

When the day of Pentecost came, they were all together in one place. Suddenly a sound like the blowing of a violent wind came from heaven and filled the whole house where they were sitting. They saw what seemed to be tongues of fire that separated and came to rest on each of them. All of them were filled with the Holy Spirit and began to speak in other tongues as the Spirit enabled them . . .

Then Peter stood up with the Eleven, raised his voice and addressed the crowd: 'Fellow Jews and all of you who are in Jerusalem, let me explain this to you; listen carefully to what I say. These men are not drunk, as you suppose. It's only nine in the morning! No, this is what was spoken by the prophet Joel:

> "In the last days, God says,
>     I will pour out my Spirit on all people.
> Your sons and daughters will prophesy,
>     your young men will see visions,
>     your old men will dream dreams.
> Even on my servants, both men and women,
>     I will pour out my Spirit in those days,
>     and they will prophesy." . . .

'Men of Israel, listen to this: Jesus of Nazareth was a man accredited by God to you by miracles, wonders and signs, which God did among you through him, as you yourselves know. This man was handed over to you by God's set purpose and foreknowledge; and you, with the help of wicked men, put him to death by nailing him to the cross. But God raised him from the dead, freeing him from the agony of death, because it was impossible for death to keep its hold on him . . .

'God has raised this Jesus to life, and we are all witnesses of the fact. Exalted to the right hand of God, he has received from the Father the promised Holy Spirit and has poured out what you now see and hear . . . Therefore let all Israel be assured of this: God has made this Jesus, whom you crucified, both Lord and Christ.'

When the people heard this, they were cut to the heart and said to Peter and the other apostles, 'Brothers, what shall we do?'

Peter replied, 'Repent and be baptised, every one of you, in the name of Jesus Christ so that your sins may be forgiven. And you will receive the gift of the Holy Spirit. The promise is for you and your children and for all who are far off – for all whom the Lord our God will call.'

With many other words he warned them; and he pleaded with

8

them, 'Save yourselves from this corrupt generation.' Those who accepted his message were baptised, and about three thousand were added to their number that day.

The Father sent Jesus Christ into the world, and Jesus Christ sends the disciples into the world. The root of the word 'mission' means 'to send'. But why send anyone?

When people ask Gavin, 'How do you understand mission?' he says, 'I understand mission from the very first words in the Bible. 'In the beginning God created . . .' We have a God who didn't keep himself to himself. We have a God of love who went out to create a world and to create people – and he created us in order to love us, and so that we could love him and one another.

We all have an image of God, and we talk about reverencing God and respecting God. But we need to get that image right, otherwise we are reverencing a false God or an idol. We need to see what God is really like – and when we see clearly we shall realize that to be godly is to be outgoing.

Some of our views of what it means to be godly are incorrect. We think of ourselves as being 'godly' when our worship is intensely private. We take the 'me and my communion' attitude, and we go to an eight o'clock service of Holy Communion in the early morning and rush out afterwards before anyone can speak to us.

If a new vicar suggests that at 'the Peace' in Holy Communion we might actually *touch* someone and shake them by the hand we shudder, and keep our arm rigid by its side and stare stolidly ahead of us while the greetings go on all round us. We like the definition of religion which someone once gave as 'The flight of the alone to the Alone'.

But to be godly, or like God, is to be very public. The Father

9

sent Jesus. Jesus, like the Father, sends his disciples: 'As the Father sent me, so I send you.' The only Christianity that exists is a Christianity about people being sent and people going out – not about people withdrawing and coming in. The greatest summary of the good news that there has ever been explains the reason for the sending and the purpose of it:

John 3:16–17
NIV

God so loved the world that he gave his one and only Son, that whoever believes in him shall not perish but have eternal life. For God did not send his Son into the world to condemn the world, but to save the world through him.

That is what our gospel is, and the task of the Decade for Evangelism is to help people to discover it for themselves. We start our Christian life by coming to Christ, when we hear Jesus calling us to come to him and to follow him. But then he sends us out in his name to love and to heal the world that he loves and died for. He won't send many of us to the other side of the world – though he will send some. The command

10

and the promise that we looked at earlier in this chapter, that Jesus gave to his disciples, was that 'You will receive power when the Holy Spirit comes on you; and you will be my witnesses *in Jerusalem*, and in all Judaea, and Samaria, and to the ends of the earth.'

Jerusalem was where they started from, and it was where they were when he spoke to them. Mission starts where we are and in the place where we live: in our family and in our friendships and in the places where we work and the places where we play.

The way to do it, however, isn't to buttonhole people and ram the gospel down their throats, so that we get the gospel and ourself a bad reputation – and so that when people see us coming they suddenly remember something very urgent that they have to do and make off at full speed in the opposite direction!

A man where I once worked used to inflict his version of the gospel on me in that sort of way. I would sit down in the cafeteria and my heart would sink as I saw him bearing down on me. I hadn't long been a Christian myself, and he abused this knowledge by talking to me very loudly about Jesus – in the hope that the people at the next tables would hear him and be converted. Needless to say they weren't.

But a year or two after that I was almost as insensitive. I was living with my parents at the time, and had been to some classes at my church on 'How to share your faith'. So I decided to share mine with our next-door neighbour Audrey when we were chatting over the fence one day. She was very put out and offended and complained about me to my mother.

A year later, though, Audrey had to have major surgery, and soon after that she *asked* me to tell her about the Christian faith. She listened with deep interest, and soon after that became a Christian herself.

'Always be prepared to give an answer *to everyone who asks you* to give a reason for the hope that you have' is the best advice to follow. If we wait until they ask, then we shall be speaking to a heart that God has been working in, and it will be like planting seeds in good soil.

But no one else asked me to give a reason for the hope that was in me. I longed to tell them, and I believed that Jesus had called me and promised me that I would tell them. But I had forgotten (or perhaps never noticed) that he had said to the disciples that they would be his witnesses in the power of his Spirit. That power is as vital to evangelism as wind is to a sailing boat. Unless the wind blows we can't get going.

I discovered this through an encounter that was almost as difficult and humiliating for me as it must have been for Naaman, when Elisha told him that if he wanted his leprosy to be healed he must go and wash seven times in the River Jordan. Naaman was very angry and went off in a rage: 'Are not Abana and Pharpar, the rivers of Damascus, better than any of the waters of Israel? Couldn't I wash in them and be cleansed?' But his servants persuaded him to submit, and because he did, he got what he wanted and his leprosy was healed. (The full story is in 2 Kings chapter 5.)

What I wanted was to be able to talk to other people about Christ. A minister I knew, David MacInnes, was talking to other people about him all the time, and I deeply coveted his gift – not in the sense of wanting to take it away from him, but of wanting to have the same gift myself. All the lovely things that I knew about Christ were locked up inside me, and I couldn't find the key to let them out.

One night I went to a charismatic prayer meeting that I didn't like at all. I didn't like the way Mrs X was running the meeting, and I frowned disapprovingly when she said, 'Yes, I know it says in 1 Corinthians 14:27 that only two or three people are to speak in a tongue, and only one at a time – but we're all friends here, so go ahead and do what you like.' What broke out was a gentle babbling all over the hall, and it went on for a long time.

Later in the evening the friend I was sitting next to, Diana, asked me if I would like Mrs X to lay hands on me. I said 'No', very firmly, but then (feeling a bit guilty that I might be blocking the blessing for everyone else in some way) said, 'Can't you do it?'

That was enough for Diana. 'I haven't got the gift,' she said, 'I will go and get Mrs X.' When Mrs X arrived she looked me in the eye and asked, 'Have you been baptised with the Holy Spirit?' I looked Mrs X back in the eye and said 'Yes'.

This all happened at the time when the charismatic movement had just reached the mainstream churches, and the churches that I went to (I worked at St Helen's, Bishopsgate and worshipped at All Souls, Langham Place, London) taught that the baptism of the Spirit happened at the moment of conversion.

But whatever people called it, something seemed to be happening in some of the mainstream churches that was making them even more alive than they had been before, and some churches that had been half dead were coming to life. Whatever it was, I knew I wanted it.

Mrs X then demanded to know if I spoke in tongues. 'No', was the answer to that. Whereupon I had to kneel down, and Mrs X laid her hands on my head. She started to shake me, exhorting God as she did so to pour out his Holy Spirit. Then she started to exhort me: 'Let the tongue flow . . . let it flow . . .' I clamped my mouth tight shut and felt horribly embarrassed. I prayed to God inside my head: 'Oh God, please make her go away . . . please!'

But there was another gift that I did want, so I asked God for that: 'If you want to give me the gift of tongues, that's fine . . . But what I really want is to be able to talk to other people about Christ the way that David MacInnes can talk to them.'

Mrs X was still shaking me and pressing her hands heavily down on my head, but she changed her exhortation: 'Praise him!' she said, 'Praise him!' I returned to my passionate prayer that God would make her go away. Then Diana whispered helpfully in my ear, 'Start praising him in English.' So I managed to squeeze out a strangled 'Hallelujah' – and my prayer was answered and Mrs X went away.

14

But strangely, in spite of everything, my other prayer was granted as well – and in an even better way than I had dared to hope. It wasn't that I was able to talk to other people about Christ because I was able to start off a conversation with them. It was that almost everyone I knew started conversations with me – and our talk flowed as freely as a mountain stream.

The gift that I didn't particularly want also came with the package, and I have to confess that I have neglected it ever since – rather as we do with Christmas presents we would never have chosen for ourselves. I have put the gift of tongues away in a cupboard and I hardly ever use it. But because of what people have said to me in the last few months I realize that I shall have to get it out and give it a proper place of honour in my life.

It was only after Jackie Pullinger had used her gift of tongues to pray every day that God sent her to the walled city in Hong Kong to do that incredible work for him amongst the gangsters, prostitutes and drug addicts so that they came out of the horror and darkness of their own lives into the glory and light of a new life in Christ. The work is still going on and they are still coming 'out of darkness into his wonderful light' (1 Peter 2:9 NIV).

But the gift of tongues is not for everyone. It isn't now and it wasn't at the start of things. Paul wrote about it to the Christians in Corinth:

**1 Corinthians 12:27–31 NIV** Now you are the body of Christ, and each one of you is a part of it. And in the church God has appointed first of all apostles, second prophets, third teachers, then workers of miracles, also those having gifts of healing, those able to help others, those with gifts of administration, and those speaking in different kinds of tongues. Are all apostles? Are all prophets? Are all teachers? Do all work miracles? Do all have gifts of healing? Do all speak in tongues? Do all interpret? But eagerly desire the greater gifts.

But the greatest gift of all is God himself – and we have only to ask to be given it. The forgiveness of our sins comes first – and we have only to ask to be given that. In chapter 11 of Luke's gospel the disciples ask Jesus to teach them how to pray, and he begins with 'Father, hallowed be your name', and goes on to tell them how to ask and what to ask for – and tells them that because the Father in heaven is the giver then they will be granted their request. And what was true for them is just as true for us.

**Luke 11:9–13 (Amplified New Testament)** So I say to you, Ask and keep on asking, and it shall be given you; seek and keep on seeking, and you shall find; knock and keep on knocking, and the door shall be opened to you. For every one who asks and keeps on asking receives, and he who seeks and keeps on seeking finds, and to him who knocks and keeps on knocking the door shall be opened. What father among you, if his son asks for a loaf of bread, will give him a stone; or if he asks for a fish, will

16

instead of a fish give him a serpent; or if he asks for an egg, will give him a scorpion? If you then, evil-minded as you are, know how to give good gifts – gifts that are to advantage – to your children, how much more will your heavenly Father give the Holy Spirit to those who ask and continue to ask Him!

That translation from the *Amplified New Testament* shows us what the verses really mean, because it indicates what the tenses are of the verb 'to ask'. It is a continual asking; the 'continuance is in the present imperative and present participles often repeated'. We have to ask and go on asking, day by day, so that the Spirit flows into us day by day like a river, and blazes day by day in our hearts to keep them on fire for God.

When we ask like that, then the Father will give us the Spirit. Then we shall be able to witness to Christ in the power of the Holy Spirit. We may find that it is fairly unlikely people who are drawn to Christ – and sometimes churchgoers can be like the people that Paul writes about to Timothy, 'holding the form of religion but denying the power of it' (2 Timothy 3:5 RSV). It happened in Jesus' day and it still happens in ours, and he told the parable of the Pharisee and the Tax Collector to warn us about it:

To some who were confident of their own righteousness and looked down on everybody else, Jesus told this parable:

Luke 18:9–14 NIV

'Two men went up to the temple to pray, one a Pharisee and the other a tax collector. The Pharisee stood up and prayed about [or to] himself: "God, I thank you that I am not like other men – robbers, evildoers, adulterers – or even like this tax collector. I fast twice a week and give a tenth of all I get."

'But the tax collector stood at a distance. He would not even look up to heaven, but beat his breast and said, "God, have mercy on me, a sinner."

'I tell you that this man, rather than the other, went home justified before God. For everyone who exalts himself will be humbled, and he who humbles himself will be exalted.'

The religious people didn't like the way Jesus mixed with the people who weren't religious, and they complained about it. But the sinners knew their need and the self-righteous didn't.

Luke 5:27–32 NIV Jesus went out and saw a tax collector by the name of Levi sitting at his tax booth. 'Follow me,' Jesus said to him, and Levi got up, left everything and followed him.

Then Levi held a great banquet for Jesus at his house, and a large crowd of tax collectors and others were eating with them. But the Pharisees and the teachers of the law who belonged to their sect complained to his disciples, 'Why do you eat and drink with tax collectors and sinners?'

Jesus answered them, 'It is not the healthy who need a doctor, but the sick. I have not come to call the righteous, but sinners to repentance.'

The people who knew they were sinners came to Jesus then and they still come. Prostitutes and drug addicts and gangsters out in Hong Kong. Criminals in Strangeways Prison in Manchester, where the terrible riots took place in 1990. And whenever and however they come they are accepted, just as they are, and forgiven, and given eternal life.

Luke 23:32–33; 39–43 NIV Two other men, both criminals, were also led out with him to be executed. When they came to the place called the Skull, there they crucified him, along with the criminals – one on his right, the other on his left . . .

One of the criminals who hung there hurled insults at him: 'Aren't you the Christ? Save yourself and us!'

But the other criminal rebuked him. 'Don't you fear God,' he said, 'since you are under the same sentence? We are punished justly, for we are getting what our deeds deserve. But this man has done nothing wrong.'

Then he said, 'Jesus, remember me when you come into your kingdom.'

Jesus answered him, 'I tell you the truth, today you will be with me in paradise.'

Derek Worlock, Roman Catholic Archbishop of Liverpool, has a lovely story to tell about a man who came to God in the last moments of his life.

When visiting a clinic one day, the priest who served as chaplain was told of the admission of a patient, renowned for a way of life which made him notorious in certain sections of the Sunday newspapers. It seemed that he was now incurably ill and had only a short time to live. The nurses were concerned for their patient, beset by the attentions of the popular Press. A few days later, when he arrived at the clinic, the priest was told that this dying man had asked to see him. When he looked into the room the man in bed, surrounded by flowers and messages, told the priest that he wished to become a member of the Church. Not surprisingly the priest was cautious. Was the man already baptised? 'No, please baptise me,' was the reply. 'It's not as simple as that,' explained the priest, scared of the man's passing emotions. 'I'll look in tomorrow and we'll have a talk.'

Next day the patient would brook no delay. 'But what about your beliefs?' asked the priest; 'I know you are very ill but belief is important for a Christian.' At the back of his mind was the thought of what the sensational Press would make of any apparent death-bed conversion, and the likely suggestion of pressure on the dying man. Then from the bed came a profession of faith: 'Don't ask me in detail. I believe what those nurses believe,' he said, pointing to a couple of Irish nurses by the door. 'All I know is that they're the best people I have ever met in my life. I want to finish up like that. I believe what they believe. Now baptise me.'

His wish was granted. A few days later, when the more sensational newspapers were recounting the man's more outrageous scandals of the past, the new Christian, a rosary round his neck, with his two nurses holding either hand, and serene in his final moments, went to God.

Derek Worlock and David Sheppard, *With Christ in the Wilderness*


*Group material, meditation and prayers for chapter 1:*
WHERE THE SHINING STARTS

*A Prayer for the Decade of Evangelism*

> Infinite Lord and eternal God,
> Rouse your Church in this land,

Restore your people's sense of mission,
And revive your work in holiness and strength.
By your Spirit, teach us to give our energy,
Our time, our money, our service and our prayer,
That your kingdom may be advanced
Here and in all the world;
In the name of Jesus Christ our Lord.

The Church in Wales

1. Read out 1 John 1 slowly, and suggest that people shut their eyes as they listen. Have at least a minute or two (time it if you aren't used to silences!) to reflect on it.
2. Ask each person to say why they have come to this group and what they hope will happen because of it. Spend some time talking about people's hopes.
3. Read out the extracts from Acts 2:1–41. Discuss, and/or ask each person to say what particular thing spoke to their heart.
4. Read out Luke 18:9–14 and Luke 5:27–32 with a pause between them (they are out of order and not consecutive readings). Then discuss the question: 'What is our gospel?'

*Meditation*

Shut your eyes and be quiet and relaxed . . . get yourself comfortable . . . and let your back be straight . . . with your hands on your knees, and your feet flat on the floor . . . be aware of the chair you are sitting on . . . there, supporting you . . . be aware of your breathing . . . be aware of the people around you, and the noises around you . . . in the room and outside it . . . all part of the world that God has made . . . every thing in it and every creature in it . . . Remember that God loves the world . . . and every creature and every thing in it . . . But things aren't as they should be and people aren't as they should be . . . our relationships have gone wrong . . . our relationship with God . . . our relationships with one another

... our relationship with the creatures and with the earth itself ... There is a darkness over the earth ... a spiritual darkness and a moral darkness ...

This is the message we have heard from him and declare to you: God is light; in him there is no darkness at all. If we claim to have fellowship with him yet walk in the darkness, we lie and do not live by the truth. But if we walk in the light, as he is in the light, we have fellowship with one another, and the blood of Jesus, his Son, purifies us from all sin. <sub>1 John 1:5–7 NIV</sub>

The light shines in the darkness, but the darkness has not understood it ... <sub>John 1–5 NIV</sub>

[Jesus said] 'I am the light of the world. Whoever follows me will never walk in darkness, but will have the light of life' ... <sub>John 8:12 NIV</sub>

[Jesus said] 'You are the light of the world. A city on a hill cannot be hidden. Neither do people light a lamp and put it under a bowl. Instead they put it on its stand, and it gives light to everyone in the house. In the same way, let your light shine before men, that they may see your good deeds and praise your Father in heaven' ... <sub>Matthew 5:14–16 NIV</sub>

Have a three- or four-minute silence and then ask people to pray their own prayers aloud, if they wish to.

## Final reading and prayer

Ask people to be quiet and to close their eyes, if they will. Then read out Isaiah 60:1–3 NIV:

> Arise, shine, for your light has come,
>     and the glory of the Lord rises upon you.
> See, darkness covers the earth
>     and thick darkness is over the peoples,
> but the Lord rises upon you
>     and his glory appears over you.
> Nations will come to your light,
>     and kings to the brightness of your dawn.

As a final prayer, the Collect for Epiphany, from the *Alternative Service Book 1980.*

> Eternal God,
> who by the shining of a star
> led the wise men to the worship of your Son:
> guide by his light the nations of the earth,
> that the whole world may behold your glory;
> through Jesus Christ our Lord.    Amen

# 2. The Church – Them and Us

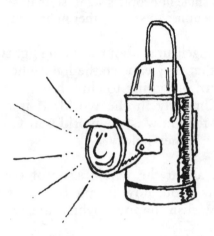

In 1983 Murray Watts wrote a short dramatic sketch about going to church. Each Christian had his or her own electric light bulb, and every Sunday morning everyone went into a building and plugged their bulbs into a special circuit. The lights were all shining nice and brightly, and they went on

shining for about an hour. Then their owners unplugged them and went home again.

Matthew
5:14–16 NJB
You are light for the world. A city built on a hill-top cannot be hidden. No one lights a lamp to put it under a tub: they put it on the lamp-stand where it shines for everyone in the house. In the same way your light must shine in people's sight, so that, seeing your good works, they may give praise to your Father in heaven.

The Decade of Evangelism is about us being lights that shine in people's sight, so that they can see the light wherever they are. One of the results of our going to church ought to be that our light burns more brightly in the world. If it only shines in church on Sunday then how is the world that God loves going to see it and see the Father's glory?

We need to think about the whole issue of going to church before we can think about how people become Christians and how to make evangelism happen, which are what the rest of this book is about.

## More than a building

When Paul wrote that 'Christ loved the church and sacrificed himself for her' (Ephesians 5:25 NJB) he wasn't talking about the building down the road that always seems to be having appeals for its roof.

If we dig back into the past to find the origins of our English word 'church' we shall discover that it comes from the Greek word *kyriakos* – 'of the lord'. *Kyrios* means 'lord and master' – and when the New Testament talks about the church it means the people of God, for whom Christ is their Saviour and Lord.

*Ekklesia*, which means 'that which is called out', is another

24

word that English versions of the New Testament translate as
'church'. Christ calls people to follow him, and those of us who
do follow are his church. Those who are called out by Christ.
The people of God.

You are a chosen race, a kingdom of priests, a holy nation, a people $\qquad$ 1 Peter 2:9 – 10
to be a personal possession to sing the praises of God who called you NJB
out of the darkness into his wonderful light. Once you were a non-
people and now you are the People of God; once you were outside
his pity; now you have received pity.

## Going to church

The trouble is that when we talk about 'going to church' what
we are often thinking of is going to the building. We know that
the people of God will be there. We shall sit alongside other
Christians in the pews or in the chairs. We shall hear the Bible
read out to us and preached on. Many of us will share in the
sacrament of bread and wine that Christ gave to us the night
before he died, when he said to the eleven disciples, 'Take, eat,
this is my body . . . Drink this, all of you, in remembrance of
me.'

But we come into church and go out again and don't talk very
much to one another. It can seem a far cry from the New
Testament's description of the early church and the three
thousand who were converted on the day of Pentecost:

They met constantly to hear the apostles teach, and to share the $\qquad$ Acts 2:42–43,
common life, to break bread, and to pray. A sense of awe was 46–47 NEB
everywhere . . . With one mind they kept up their daily attendance at
the temple, and, breaking bread in private houses, shared their meals
with unaffected joy, as they praised God and enjoyed the favour of
the whole people. And day by day the Lord added to their number
those whom he was saving.

In the group discussion material at the end of this chapter one
of the questions we shall be asking everyone to think about is:

25

'Why do I go to church – and what happens when I am there?' There will be a cluster of questions that we shall probably ask ourselves while we are wondering what the main answer is.

Do I go to worship God in a way that is different from the way I worship when I'm not in church?

Do I go to get strength to live the week ahead – and do I get more strength through being in church than I would if I just prayed on my own?

Do I go just because it makes me feel better – and if I come out not feeling better, do I then think that it hasn't been a very good service?

Most of us find that the sheer act of praising God together with other Christians will increase our faith, so we shall go out of church enthusiastic for God. Then our light will be shining in the right places and we shall be loving the world in the right sense. We shall bind up its wounds, fight for social justice, feed the people who are hungry and clothe the people who are naked, and tell them of the love and forgiveness of God in Christ.

## Tares and wheat

Churchgoers are often criticized by people in the world and accused of being hypocrites, and all too often their accusers are right.

The explanation is that there are tares as well as wheat growing in the Church – people who practise the outward form of religion but don't have the inner life. They are Christians in name only. Christ said it would be so, and that on the judgement day they would be rooted out and burnt because they were useless and fruitless:

The kingdom of Heaven may be compared to a man who sowed Matthew 13:24–30 NJB good seed in his field. While everybody was asleep his enemy came, sowed darnel all among the wheat, and made off. When the new wheat sprouted and ripened, then the darnel appeared as well.

The owner's labourers went to him and said, 'Sir, was it not good seed that you sowed in your field? If so, where does the darnel come from?'

He said to them, 'Some enemy has done this.'

And the labourers said, 'Do you want us to go and weed it out?' But he said, 'No, because when you weed out the darnel you might pull up the wheat with it. Let them both grow till the harvest; and at harvest time I shall say to the reapers: First collect the darnel and tie it in bundles to be burnt, then gather the wheat into my barn.'

The darnel (tares) that Jesus talks about is a particular 'deleterious grass (*lolium temulentum*) which grows as a weed among corn' (*Shorter Oxford Dictionary*), and 'deleterious' means harmful. But in their early stages, when they first sprout out of the ground, both plants look the same. It is when they are full grown that the difference is obvious. The wheat has grown an ear of grain, but the darnel hasn't. It couldn't have, because it has a different nature from the wheat.

The different and wonderful thing about being a Christian is that we share in the divine nature.

## Sharing the nature of God

Simon Peter, servant and apostle of Jesus Christ, to those who have 2 Peter 1:1–4 NJB received a faith as precious as our own, given through the saving justice of our God and Saviour Jesus Christ. Grace and peace be yours in abundance through the knowledge of our Lord.

By his divine power, he has lavished on us all the things we need for life and for true devotion, through the knowledge of him who has called us by his own glory and goodness. Through these, the greatest and priceless promises have been lavished on us, that through them

27

you should share the divine nature and escape the corruption rife in the world through disordered passion.

We don't always appreciate or realize all that we have in Christ! In *Mr Jones, Meet the Master*, Catherine Marshall puts a quote from *Pastor's Postscript* at the start of one of the chapters: 'Church members in too many cases are like deep sea divers, encased in the suits designed for many fathoms deep, marching bravely to pull out plugs in bath tubs.' Church members like that have never grown up in their faith. They are like stunted plants, or children who have never matured. They should have done, and the New Testament tells them off:

**Hebrews 5:12–14 RSV** For though by this time you ought to be teachers, you need someone to teach you again the first principles of God's word. You need milk, not solid food; for every one who lives on milk is unskilled in the

28

word of righteousness, for he is a child. But solid food is for the mature, for those who have their faculties trained by practice to distinguish good from evil.

If those of us who do go to church take seriously the need to grow up to Christian maturity, so that we can tell other people what our faith means to us and explain it to them, then the Decade of Evangelism will be a success.

The Decade isn't about getting people to come to church. It is about people getting to know Christ. But nevertheless they will almost certainly end up coming to church, because to become a Christian is to become a member of the church. Members of the church of Christ also go to the building that we call church – even though for some of them 'going to church' is going to a house church in someone's home.

In England only 10 per cent of people go to church.

## Why people don't go to church

There are various reasons why people don't go to church. For some, life is about facts and material things and they seem to have no awareness of its spiritual and religious dimensions. On the whole our society doesn't think that God has anything to do with anything that happens. Matters to do with God are not seen as being matters of *fact*, but as matters of opinion. People will say, 'Well, if that's your opinion, fine! If you want to be a Christian, fine! That's your opinion – but it's your private opinion. Not mine.'

A hundred years ago many people hardly realized that there

were any other religions in the world as well as Christianity. But now we have been exposed to other religious insights. People of other faiths live on our doorstep, and television tells us about other faiths. So we are aware that God is a disputed area. That tends to affect the credibility of Christianity – or at least it affects people's readiness to accept that one area or another has got all the answers.

Truth is regarded as relative, not absolute or independent, and not everyone is very good at thinking logically about the truth. But either there is a God or there isn't. If there is, then saying that there isn't won't make him cease to be. If God is like Jesus said he was – a loving father who longs for his son in the far country to come home again – then either Jesus was right or he was wrong. If he was right, then any religion which says otherwise is wrong.

Another reason why people aren't going to church is that we are suffering from the legacy of thirty years' abandonment of outreach to children. In the 1950s, 55 per cent of the parents in Britain were sending their children to Sunday school. And in the early 1950s, 83 per cent of a sample of adults over sixteen interviewed said that for a considerable number of their younger years they were members of a Sunday school. But today the number of children going to Sunday school or to church-related activities is only about 15 per cent.

The church in the old days never had to work hard in order to get children to come to Sunday school. They just came. So when they stopped coming, the church didn't know what to do. It had never analysed why they came, so it didn't know what things it might do in order to encourage them to come again. It is now discovering these things, and in some places there are large and flourishing Sunday schools and holiday clubs.

The church has largely failed to realize how much it has relied on the fact that the children understood its special vocabulary. Children had listened to the stories, so they knew what the words meant. There were stories about forgiveness, and they knew about the dying thief. So they had some shadowy awareness of what forgiveness meant. So when, later on in their life, perhaps much later, someone preached about forgiveness, the whole thing would come alive.

That does not happen any more. Whole generations of children are given religious education in school, but they hardly know anything about the Bible. Some young people know the name 'Jesus', and 'Christ', only as swear words. They know nothing about his life or his death.

## No golden age

Sometimes we get depressed about the fact that most people don't go to church. But we need to get rid of the idea that once there was a golden age when most people did. There has never been an age when the church was packed, and there have been other ages when church attendance was proportionally a good deal less than it is now.

When John Wesley formed his Holy Club, he did it because the church was corrupt. He faced a situation in which the church was totally in the power of the privileged and was part of the establishment. It was the time of the 'hunting parson' – not a man of God, but a horseman!

When we look at the big, beautiful churches that were built with the wealth that came from Britain's wool (the Lord Chancellor's Woolsack dates back to those days) we may imagine that they needed to be big to pack in all the people who wanted to come week by week. But in fact they were built more to glorify man than God.

At the time of the Evangelical Awakening in the eighteenth century, Christians were very despondent about the small attendances in church.

The working classes have never been strong in the Church of England. At the time of the Industrial Revolution the church was seen as the preserve of the landowners and the mill owners. Sometimes the workers did go to church, but only because their employer would sack them if they didn't. The working classes were alienated from the church because they were treated so badly by the church-going industrialists. Charles Kingsley's books *Alton Lock* and *The Water Babies* give a contemporary and terrible account of what life was like for the poor.

In later Victorian times the churches often did fine work amongst the poor, but the poor were always on the receiving end of their largesse. They were the people who 'needed to be helped'. But people don't usually like being beholden to somebody else. So when they got a bit more prosperous they abandoned the church along with the soup kitchen and stayed at home.

In the Anglican Church there is the additional problem of our very literary set-up. We have a beautiful liturgy, but a lot of people can't understand it. It is very wordy, and a lot of the words are long. The churches that did make some progress with the less educated and the less privileged were non-Anglican.

Methodism grew out of the small groups of ordinary, under-privileged people that formed its early class meetings – and like attracts like. We all feel comfortable with other people like ourselves. And the Methodists were known for their enthusiasm and their rousing hymns.

The Roman Catholic Church also had an impact on the working classes, and it has been the most successful of all the churches in reaching the different segments of society and to some extent holding them in tension. There is a beautifully colourful ritual, and a lot to watch – and it is almost always done beautifully.

Perhaps one of the Roman Catholic Church's greatest strengths is its emphasis on the confessional. People can confess their sins to the priest and be assured that their sins are forgiven – and there is no more healing thing that can ever happen to any human being than to know that his or her sins have been forgiven.

Protestants believe that we can go direct to God the Father through God the Son, the one and only mediator between God and man, to confess our sins and be forgiven. And some of us may be less than happy about the penances that are imposed in the Catholic Church, because we would want to say that the forgiveness comes utterly through the grace and love of God and the atoning work of Christ on the Cross. But the penances are not usually very heavy, and they are not about getting the sins forgiven but about showing God that one is truly penitent.

Before I was born my parents lived for many years in Italy, and my mother used to tell me how on Saturday night and Sunday morning she would see the prostitutes going into the con-fessional box in the cathedral in Milan. Then, on Sunday night, she would see them going out to work on the streets again.

But perhaps the compassion that Jesus showed to prostitutes should make us wary of condemning such easy forgiveness – and help us to understand the desperation that sometimes drives a woman to sell her body to a man for money.

In England the Salvation Army had a powerful impact on the poor and the underprivileged – and General William Booth fought a mighty campaign against Parliament on behalf of child prostitutes and won it. Some of the MPs had actually been using the child prostitutes – and it isn't surprising that over the years outsiders have seen churchgoers as hypocritical. Like the mill owners and the mine owners and the landowners, many Members of Parliament were churchgoers who didn't care about morality or social justice. Booth won his campaign in the teeth of their resistance.

## 'The church of the unchurched'

Gerald Priestland, one-time Religious Affairs Correspondent of the BBC, used to talk about 'the church of the unchurched'. What he meant by it was that all over Britain (and the more so the further we go north) we find a large number of people who would be quite offended if we said we didn't think they were Christians. They pray from time to time (according to a recent survey 40 per cent of the population of Britain pray) but they don't go to church.

In one sense this is something we can find encouraging, and Gavin's personal view is that it doesn't mean that we have only to find the right tactics and then we shall get them to come to church. Rather, that since there are a lot of believing, praying people who never come to church (and probably never will come) then we ought to be doing all we can to nurture their faith.

In the past we nurtured it by building so much into the children. Because of what they learnt in Sunday school they knew it for the rest of their lives and they brought their children up on it. This could mean that in the Decade of Evangelism we ought to try to build up the work that we do with children, and also try to keep (and if possible improve) religious television and radio.

The medium of broadcasting is one of the ways in which the church of the unchurched is nurtured. They are the people who watch 'Songs of Praise'. But on the whole that church is growing old. There probably aren't many recruits for the church of the unchurched joining in their twenties and thirties. They are growing out – rather as a hair tint or a perm grows out – and unless we can do something about it they will have grown right out in fifty years.

But one church is the fastest growing in the world. At the beginning of this century the Pentecostal Church came to birth in California. It has now spread all over the world and has millions of members. It is decidedly working class, with much more immediacy about its services. The people get emotional about their religion and express their feelings enthusiastically, and their music is as far removed from traditional church music as the Equator is from the North Pole.

But right at the heart of the Pentecostal revival is reliance on the work of the Holy Spirit. That takes us back to our last chapter – and the fact that when the church moves out into the world in the power of the Holy Spirit, she will be an effective witness to Christ and people will believe.

If it seems to you that the Church as organised has somehow lost its sense of proportion, remember that only through the Church has the Gospel ever reached you, and that only through the Church can it reach the ages far ahead. And you will do more to the cause of Christ by bringing what reality you can into its life than you can ever render by staying outside and doing what seems possible to you, or you and your few friends, in isolation.

William Temple, *Christian Faith and Life*


*Group material, meditation and prayers for chapter 2:*
THE CHURCH – THEM AND US

*A Prayer for the Decade of Evangelism*

Almighty God, you have called your Church to preach the gospel to all nations, and you have taught us to seek and serve Christ in all people. Strengthen and inspire the congregations of this church as we prepare for a Decade of Evangelism. Help us to recognize the

36

promptings of the Spirit in those who do not now profess the Name of your Christ, and, by our words and deeds, to encourage them in their pilgrimage; that they may find the joy and peace of knowing Jesus Christ, their Lord and ours; who lives and reigns with you and the Holy Spirit, now and for ever.    Amen

The Episcopal Church in the USA

Read out the following questions (which appeared in this chapter) one by one, and after each one ask a few people to share their answer with the rest of the group:

1. Do you go to church to worship God in a way that is different from your weekday worship?
2. Do you go to church to get strength to live the week ahead – and do you think you get more strength through being in church than you would if you simply prayed on your own?
3. Do you go to church just because it makes you feel better – and if you don't come out feeling better, do you then think that it hasn't been a very good service?

Suggest that people shut their eyes, and then read out 2 Peter 1:1–4 slowly, with silences between the sentences and a slightly longer silence at the end. Then read out the quotation from *Pastor's Postscript*:

Church members in too many cases are like deep sea divers, encased in the suits designed for many fathoms deep, marching bravely to pull out plugs in bath tubs.

Ask people if they agree with that, and ask them to think about the enormous riches we have in Christ – and to share what they think. How much does it mean to them that we 'share the divine nature'? Ask them to share any doubts and difficulties they have about the passage from 2 Peter.

Ask people if it depresses them that church attendance is so low. Does it matter? Is there anything we can do about it? Do we need to repent of past and present injustices?

37

Discuss this quotation from George Appleton's *Journey for a Soul*:

The Church is the community of the Spirit, not as having a monopoly of the Spirit, but as having been called into existence by God and entrusted with the word and the sacraments. In the Church there should be going on in a concentrated way the work of the Spirit, which in a diffuse way is going on throughout creation. When the Church is truly the Church it is introducing a new dimension into the social situation, thus giving hope for an eventual transformation.

As a final meditation, ask people to sit comfortably in their chairs, with their hands on their knees and their eyes shut. Ask them to listen, and to pray that as they do, God will speak to their hearts. Ask them to be especially aware of the shining of light in this passage they are going to hear. Be still for a moment. Then, slowly and with some silences, read out the words which the risen Christ spoke to the churches in Asia when he gave to John a vision on the island of Patmos:

**Revelation 1:4–6, 10–20; 3:14–20 NIV**

John, To the seven churches in the province of Asia: Grace and peace to you from him who is, and who was, and who is to come, and from the seven spirits before his throne, and from Jesus Christ, who is the faithful witness, the firstborn from the dead, and the ruler of the kings of the earth.

To him who loves us and has freed us from our sins by his blood, and has made us to be a kingdom and priests to serve his God and Father – to him be glory and power for ever and ever!

On the Lord's Day I was in the Spirit, and I heard behind me a loud voice like a trumpet, which said, 'Write on a scroll what you see and send it to the seven churches: to Ephesus, Smyrna, Pergamum, Thyatira, Sardis, Philadelphia and Laodicea.'

I turned round to see the voice that was speaking to me. And when I turned I saw seven golden lampstands, and among the lampstands was someone 'like a son of man', dressed in a robe reaching down to his feet and with a golden sash round his chest. His head and hair were white like wool, as white as snow, and his eyes were like blazing fire. His feet were like bronze glowing in a furnace, and his voice was like the sound of rushing waters. In his right hand he held seven stars

38

and out of his mouth came a sharp double-edged sword. His face was like the sun shining in all its brilliance.

When I saw him, I fell at his feet as though dead. Then he placed his right hand on me and said: 'Do not be afraid. I am the First and the Last. I am the Living One; I was dead, and behold I am alive for ever and ever! And I hold the keys of death and Hades.

'Write, therefore, what you have seen, what is now and what will take place later. The mystery of the seven stars that you saw in my right hand and of the seven golden lampstands is this: The seven stars are the angels of the seven churches, and the seven lampstands are the seven churches . . .

'To the angel of the church in Laodicea write:

'These are the words of the Amen, the faithful and true witness, the ruler of God's creation. I know your deeds, that you are neither cold nor hot. I wish you were either one or the other! So, because you are lukewarm – neither hot nor cold – I am about to spit you out of my mouth. You say, "I am rich; I have acquired wealth and do not need a thing." But you do not realise that you are wretched, pitiful, poor, blind and naked. I counsel you to buy from me gold refined in the fire, so that you can become rich, and white clothes to wear, so that you can cover your shameful nakedness, and salve to put on your eyes, so that you can see.

'Those whom I love I rebuke and discipline. So be earnest, and repent. Here I am! I stand at the door and knock. If anyone hears my voice and opens the door, I will come in and eat with him, and he with me.'

After a short silence ask people to pray their own prayers aloud, if they wish to.

## A Prayer for the Decade of Evangelism

Holy Spirit of God, all-powerful as the wind, you came to the Church on the Day of Pentecost to quicken its life and empower its witness. Come to us now as the Wind of Heaven and breathe new life into our souls; and revive your work among us, that God in all things may be glorified, through Jesus Christ our Lord.   Amen

The Church of England

# 3. Evangelism – Naturally

Most people become Christians very undramatically. That means that a lot of evangelism also happens very undramatically, and that can be quite reassuring. Most evangelism takes place without any melodrama at all, in the ordinary run of our lives, amongst the people we live and work with.

In St Mary's Church in Reigate a visiting preacher questioned people from the pulpit about how they became Christians and asked them to raise their hands.

'Did you become a Christian through hearing a sermon?' Just a few people put up their hands. 'Did you become a Christian through an evangelistic campaign?' Rather more hands went up. Then the final question: 'Did you become a Christian

40

through the influence of another person?' – and a forest of hands shot up all over the church.

Some Christian traditions see things in a different way and believe that a person becomes a Christian at their baptism. This is not the place or the book to have a theological argument – and it would be unprofitable and unwinnable anyway. But what there isn't any argument about in any of the traditions is that a Christian is meant to grow up in the Christian life, in a relationship with God that gets deeper and richer from year to year. When that happens a Christian is doing what he or she was told to do in the service of baptism. In the churches which use this lovely symbolic piece of ritual, a small candle lit from the great Easter candle is handed to the godparents, and the priest tells the infant disciple to 'Shine as a light in the world to the glory of God the Father.'

So some churches might simply see the process of evangelism as a way to help people to claim the life and the power and the riches that already belong to them but which they have never known about or used.

But whatever our churchmanship is, the practice of evangelism has to include telling people what the good news really is. Then the life of Christ will start to grow in them. They will start to 'take hold of the life which is life indeed' (1 Timothy 6:19 RSV), and realize the wonder and the power of what Jesus meant when he said, 'I came that they may have *and* enjoy life, and

41

have it in abundance – to the full, till it overflows' (John 10:10 *Amplified New Testament*).

So how are we to set about making evangelism happen? One way to find out is to look at a story which is very dramatic, but out of which we shall be able to draw some principles that are not at all dramatic. It is the story of Philip and the Ethiopian Eunuch.

Acts 9:26–40
GNB

An angel of the Lord said to Philip, 'Get ready and go south to the road that goes from Jerusalem to Gaza.' (This road is not used nowadays). So Philip got ready and went. Now an Ethiopian eunuch, who was an important official in charge of the treasury of the queen of Ethiopia, was on his way home. He had been to Jerusalem to worship God and was going back home in his carriage. As he rode along, he was reading from the book of the prophet Isaiah. The Holy Spirit said to Philip, 'Go over to that carriage and stay close to it.' Philip ran over and heard him reading from the book of the prophet Isaiah. He asked him, 'Do you understand what you are reading?'
    The official replied, 'How can I understand unless someone explains it to me?' And he invited Philip to climb up and sit in the carriage with him. The passage of scripture which he was reading was this:

> 'Like a sheep that is taken to be slaughtered,
>     like a lamb that makes no sound when its wool is cut off,
>     he did not say a word.
> He was humiliated, and justice was denied him.
>     No one will be able to tell about his descendants,
>     because his life on earth has come to an end.'

The official asked Philip, 'Tell me, of whom is the prophet saying this? Of himself or of someone else?' Then Philip began to speak; starting from this passage of scripture, he told him the Good News about Jesus. As they travelled down the road, they came to a place where there was some water, and the official said, 'Here is some water. What is to keep me from being baptized?'
    The official ordered the carriage to stop, and both Philip and the official went down into the water, and Philip baptized him. When they came up out of the water, the Spirit of the Lord took Philip

42

away. The official did not see him again, but continued on his way, full of joy. Philip found himself in Ashdod; he went on to Caesarea, and on the way he preached the Good News in every town.

There are three vital things that we can learn from this story to help us to make evangelism happen in the right way.

1. The Holy Spirit was working in the Ethiopian official and also directing Philip to the right place to find him.
2. The Ethiopian was a motivated seeker.
3. He met a motivated sharer.

There was a desire in the Ethiopian to know and to understand what he was reading about, so he was ready to respond when Philip asked him the right question. There was a desire in Philip to tell people about the good news, so when he met this man and found him reading this passage of scripture he was ready and willing to tell him what it meant. He was also able to tell him, and we have got to be able to do the same thing.

If we are going to set up some structures for evangelism, that story suggests to us the question we have to ask ourselves first. How can we bring together motivated sharers and motivated seekers, rather than letting motivated sharers charge off and waste their energy in places where nobody wants to hear them – and then perhaps discover afterwards that there had been motivated seekers in some other place with nobody there to help them?

Some years ago Gavin was talking to the minister of a well known London church which had a large and dedicated congregation with a large percentage of motivated sharers. Forty or fifty of these people regularly went out on to the streets, trying to do 'cold evangelism'. But they were getting nowhere. Gavin asked the minister: 'How many people are coming to your church now, whom you made contact with through this street evangelism?' The answer was, 'None.'

Gavin knew the area where the church was situated very well, so he asked another question. 'Surely, in your sort of set-up, with bed-sit land all around you and all the students, you must have people just dropping in to look you up and down and see what you are like?' 'Yes,' he said, 'we do. Every week.' So Gavin said, 'And what do you do about them?' He said, 'We ask them to fill up cards and hand them over ...' 'Do they?' Gavin asked. 'Yes, they are very good.' 'How many cards are we talking about?' Gavin asked. 'About twenty a week,' he said. So Gavin asked, 'And what do you do with the cards?' The minister's reply was honest but ashamed: 'I wish you hadn't asked me that!'

That church was so busy doing the sort of evangelism that wasn't working that they didn't have time to give to the mission that was happening on their doorstep with the people that God had sent to them. The fields at their feet were 'already white to harvest', but they were trying to scratch a harvest that wasn't there from the streets of London.

We need to translate into today's setting the story of Jesus sending out the apostles and saying in effect, 'Don't go from door to door. Go where there's a welcome, and stay.' That means, 'Where you're not wanted don't stay – and don't even keep the dust on your feet' (see Matthew 10:5–15).

We can also learn from the missionary tactics of St Paul. The first thing he always did was to go into the synagogue to preach – until they kicked him out. Then he would go wherever he could find common ground with people.

In Philippi he went to the place where people met to pray. In Athens he hired a lecture hall, and he spoke in the market place. He had something to say about the meaning of life, so he talked to the philosophers and was alongside them.

We have printed out these passages from the Bible at length, because they show us the way to go to the place where people are, and how to talk about the gospel to them in ways that they will understand. When Paul talked to Jews he used the Jewish scriptures. When he talked to Greeks he started where they were and went on from there, and used situations and quotations that they knew.

Paul had a vision in which he saw a Macedonian standing and begging him, 'Come over to Macedonia and help us!' As soon as Paul had this vision, we got ready to leave for Macedonia, because we decided that God had called us to preach the Good News to the people there. Acts 16:9–15 GNB
   We left by ship from Troas and sailed straight across to Samothrace, and the next day to Neapolis. From there we went inland to Philippi, a city of the first district of Macedonia; it is also a Roman colony. We spent several days there. On the Sabbath we went out of

the city to the river-side, where we thought there would be a place where Jews gathered for prayer. We sat down and talked to the women who gathered there. One of those who heard us was Lydia from Thyatira, who was a dealer in purple cloth. She was a woman who worshipped God, and the Lord opened her mind to pay attention to what Paul was saying. After she and the people of her house had been baptized, she invited us, 'Come and stay in my house if you have decided that I am a true believer in the Lord.' And she persuaded us to go.

Acts 17:1–7
GNB

Paul and Silas travelled on through Amphipolis and Apollonia and came to Thessalonica, where there was a synagogue. According to his usual habit Paul went to the synagogue. There during three Sabbaths he held discussions with the people, quoting and explaining the Scriptures and proving from them that the Messiah had to suffer and rise from death. 'This Jesus whom I announce to you,' Paul said, 'is the Messiah.' Some of them were convinced and joined Paul and Silas; so did many of the leading women and a large group of Greeks who worshipped God.

But the Jews were jealous and gathered some of the worthless loafers from the streets and formed a mob. They set the whole city in an uproar and attacked the home of a man called Jason, in an attempt to find Paul and Silas and bring them out to the people. But when they did not find them they dragged Jason and some other believers before the city authorities and shouted, 'These men have caused trouble everywhere! Now they have come to our city, and Jason has kept them in his house. They are all breaking the laws of the Emperor, saying that there is another king, whose name is Jesus.'

Acts 17:16–28
GNB

While Paul was waiting in Athens for Silas and Timothy, he was greatly upset when he noticed how full of idols the city was. So he held discussions in the synagogue with the Jews and with the Gentiles who worshipped God, and also in the public square every day with the people who happened to pass by. Certain Epicurean and Stoic teachers also debated with him. Some of them asked, 'What is this ignorant show-off trying to say?'

Others answered, 'He seems to be talking about foreign gods.' They said this because Paul was preaching about Jesus and the resurrection. So they took Paul, brought him before the city council, the Areopagus, and said, 'We would like to know what this new teaching is that you are talking about. [Note that *they* were asking the questions.] Some of the things we hear you say sound strange to us, and we would like to know what they mean.' (For all the citizens of Athens and the foreigners who lived there liked to spend all their time telling and hearing the latest new thing.)

Paul stood up in front of the city council and said, 'I see that in every way you Athenians are very religious. For as I walked through your city and looked at the places where you worship, I found an altar on which is written "To an Unknown God". That which you worship, then, even though you do not know it, is what I now proclaim to you. God, who made the world and everything in it, is Lord of heaven and earth and does not live in man-made temples. Nor does he need anything that we can supply by working for him, since it is he himself who gives life and breath and everything else to everyone. From one man he created all races of mankind and made them live throughout the whole earth. He himself fixed beforehand the exact times and the limits of the places where they would live. He did this so that they would look for him, and perhaps find him as they felt about for him. Yet God is actually not far from any one of us; as someone has said, "In him we live and move and exist." It is as some of your poets have said, "We too are his children." '

Paul did his evangelism in the places where people were already thinking about God (or at least about gods). We shall be sensible if we take a leaf out of his book. Far too much of our thinking about evangelism involves making plans about how we can go and canvas people from cold, people who haven't even started thinking about Christianity or about God and who aren't a bit interested. The New Testament principle is that we go where we have something to start with, because the Spirit is already at work.

When we have identified who these people are and where they are, then we have to work out the best way of getting together with them. There are really only three basic directions in which we can move. Either *we go to them* in their own homes, or *they come to us* in our church buildings or at some central spot, or somehow *we meet in the middle* in other people's homes or even in pubs.

Then we have to say 'Right, working with the way things are, what are the formats that are going to make sense for evangelism in this context?' These can vary. We might decide that a format which will make sense is to hold meetings in the church buildings. It is surprising how well that can work in an area where there is a fairly formal, 'churchy' set-up.

Another format which might work is to have supper evenings – a delicious meal in a central setting with an after-dinner speaker who speaks about the gospel. It is important that the guests know what they are coming to, and that the Christian speaker doesn't come as a total surprise/horrible shock. To force the gospel down people's throats along with their supper is totally unacceptable and appallingly rude, but unfortunately and unhappily people sometimes try to do it.

Another format would be a mixture of dialoguing and preaching. Most of Gavin's missions are like that. What he likes to do are missions where the first week is spent in people's homes, dialoguing. Not trying to push them to a decision, but just trying to get them to think. Gavin's theory is that a lot of people think about God from the teeth backwards and that it is only when they start talking that they start thinking.

One of the big problems with our society is that on the whole people just do not talk about God. Therefore they don't necessarily think very much about God. The advantage of this sort of mission, with people talking to one another, is that they stimulate one another to think even more. So what we have to do is to create occasions which help people to think aloud about their approach to God.

Billy Graham seems to be a catalyst which results in people talking to each other about God. A mission can create agendas and create talking points, and when there is something on the scale of a Billy Graham mission going on in a country, people start to talk about it. Particularly when it is backed by a publicity campaign like 'Can you make sense of Life?' (which incidentally won the *Campaign* magazine award for the best advertising campaign of 1989).

What any mission is trying to do is to encourage people to talk about themselves and about the mission. The talking process leads to the thinking process, and the thinking process can lead to the seeking process, which will mean that people start asking questions.

It is important for effective evangelism that people should feel free to ask their own questions. There is obviously a place for the proclamation of the gospel, but sometimes all that the proclamation seems to consist of is handing out the answers — like the *Peanuts* cartoon which proclaims that 'Jesus Christ is the answer', and Charlie Brown asks, 'But what is the question?' We need to wait until people ask their own questions, and a mission is a golden opportunity to get them to do that.

When we get the right mix of dialogue and proclamation then one event that can be of great value is a simple 'fun together' sort of occasion. Gavin writes about this in his book *To Reach a Nation*, and he points out that as Christians we belong to two communities. We belong to the redemption community and to the creation community, and if we restrict ourselves to living totally within the redemption community then we only have things in common with a very small section of the whole population — and our lights aren't shining where they ought to be.

The truth is that we live in both worlds and we have things in common with both worlds. Some churches run things like picnics, outings, barbecues, suppers, barn dances and so on. These can be great fun, and church people can invite their uncommitted friends to join them. These events are not meant to be evangelistic. But they are occasions when friendships are

49

deepened, and they can help to make undisguised evangelism possible at a later stage.

Sometimes in a compact community such as a small town or a village, those things happen anyway, and Christians can simply go to them (please, not keep away!). But in the featureless and often drab life of suburbia and the inner city there is no real sense of community, so a creation community event won't happen naturally. But the church is ideally placed to make it happen. As part of its own ongoing life it can gather people together just to enjoy themselves and celebrate their personhood together – and there needn't be too many hang-ups about the fact that the evening doesn't end with an Epilogue!

In a mission which Gavin was involved with in the north of England they had a Scottish dancing evening on the first night, and simply ran trailers for the mission. Five hundred people turned up to it, and in the course of the evening the organizers ran a brief trailer for the mission and told people what would be happening in the week to come. All Gavin did that first evening was to say 'Hullo' and 'Goodbye'.

A good principle to work on in evangelism is 'first the natural and then the spiritual.' Friendships first – for their own sake. Inviting people to meals and talking with them about ordinary things. Then conversations about God will naturally start to happen.

'Kindness has converted more sinners than either zeal, eloquence, or learning' (F. W. Faber).


## Group material, meditation and prayers for chapter 3:
### EVANGELISM — NATURALLY

### A Prayer for the Decade of Evangelism

Almighty God, you have called us into your service in the Church at a time of change and opportunity: give us strength and grace to see what you are calling us to be and to do. May our thankfulness for your many mercies in the past provide us with even greater willingness to seek your ways in the days ahead.

Guide us in the path of truth: lead us in our worship and preparation: draw us closer to you and to each other: help us to reach out in faith and confidence to all who seek your path; through Jesus Christ our Lord.   Amen

The Church of Ireland


1. Read out the story of Philip and the Ethiopian eunuch from Acts 9:26—40.
2. Are you a 'motivated sharer' in the sense that Philip was? Do you want to share the gospel with other people yourself?
3. Read out Acts 16:9—15 and Acts 17:1—7.
4. Are there modern equivalents of the places where Paul preached and talked to people about the gospel? If there are, how could you follow his example? If there don't seem to be any, how could you set them up? Who are the people who might be interested? We shall be looking in more detail in later chapters at possible events at which evangelism could take place — but think of ways that might work in your area.
5. What do you think about your church running events for the whole neighbourhood such as picnics, outings, barbecues,

suppers and barn dances? Divide into groups of two or three and ask each group to work out a simple plan for one of those events.

## Meditation

Ask people to sit comfortably, to shut their eyes, and to listen attentively to this reading from Metropolitan Anthony Bloom's book *God and Man*. Read it out slowly with some spaces for silence . . . [*I have put dots in place of commas to indicate the places where it would be good to pause . . .* ] and tell people before you start that it is about their response to a church service . . .

The dismissal [at the end of the service] means this: You have been on the Mount of Transfiguration . . . you have seen the glory of God . . . you have been on the road to Damascus . . . you have faced the living God . . . you have been in the upper chamber . . . you have been here and there in Galilee and Judaea, all the mysterious places where one meets God, and now having spent several days with him, he says now that so much has been given – go, your joy will never abandon you . . .

What you have acquired, you will never lose as long as you remain faithful. Go now, and if truly you have discovered joy, how can you not give joy to others? . . . If truly you have come nearer to truth, how can you keep it for yourself? . . . If truly something has been kindled in you which is life, are you going to allow anyone not to have a spark of this life? . . . It does not mean go round and tell everyone specifically religious things or use clerical phrases. It means that you should go into the world which is yours with a radiance, with a joy, with an intensity that will make everyone look at you and say, 'He has something he hadn't before. Is it that truly God has come near? He has something he never had before and which I do not possess – joy, life, certainty, a new courage, a new daring, a vision . . . where can I get it?'

People will also say to you, 'Mad you are.' I answer in those cases, and there are many, I say, 'I am mad, but one thing I find strange. You who are wise call to the mad man, and the mad man is happy, alive and you feel dead; let us share my folly . . . it is God's folly.'

You are now going to start. With God you go now, with him on all the ways, on all the roads; you can dance on the Mount of Transfiguration . . . you can bring concreteness of life for others . . . May God bless you in it with joy. I don't know any other words than 'with joy' . . . go with joy, bring joy, and then you will have brought everything else, because God is joy, he is life, he is intensity.

Spend two or three minutes in silence. Then ask people to pray their own prayers out loud, if they would like to.

*A Prayer for the Decade of Evangelism*

> Grant us, Lord God,
> the vision of your Kingdom,
> forgiveness and new life,
> and the stirring of your Spirit;
> so that we may
> share your vision,
> proclaim your love,
> and change this world,
> in the name of Christ.    Amen
> The Anglican Church of Australia

# 4. Ways to Make Evangelism Happen

There is only one absolutely sure-fire way of reaching people with the gospel, and that is to be their friend. But the friendship has to be genuine – just as love has to be: 'Let love be genuine', Paul wrote to the Christians in Rome, and if friendship or love have a hidden agenda then they aren't genuine. We must never make friends with a person simply with a view to 'winning them for Christ'. If we do we are making a fake offer to them, and it means that we know almost nothing of what true love and true friendship are about.

Joan Walsh Anglund wrote a children's book about friendship called *A Friend is Someone Who Likes You*. When someone likes us we usually know it, but not always – and sometimes people who don't know about friendship don't recognize what is being held out to them, and then we have to proceed tentatively and delicately until they know they can trust us.

Sometimes you don't know who are your friends . . . Sometimes they are there all the time, but you walk right past them and don't notice that they like you in a special way. And then you think you don't have any friends. Then you must stop hurrying and rushing so fast . . . Sometimes you have to find your friend . . . Some people have lots and lots of friends . . . and some people have quite a few friends . . . but everyone . . . everyone in the whole world has at least one friend.
Where did you find yours?

That sort of talk isn't only for children. Jesus said that we have to become as a little child in order to enter the kingdom of heaven, and the honesty that little children have is just one of the things we need to learn from them. We can be good at our job and still have an emptiness inside us that we don't even recognize. Often our striving for success is a way of crying out for recognition: 'Look what I've done and look what I've got!' But unless we have got some friends and some loving relationships we haven't really got very much.

Some people seem to have the gift of making friends, and other people need to learn how to and pray to be given the gift. Jesus had it, and people recognized it. The religious people who recognized it and didn't like it said, 'Look at this man! He is a glutton and a drunkard, a friend of tax collectors and sinners' (Luke 7:34 NJB). But some of the tax collectors and the sinners came into the kingdom through their transforming friendship with Jesus.

One of the Pharisees invited him to a meal. When he arrived at the Pharisee's house and took his place at table, suddenly a woman came in, who had a bad name in the town. She had heard he was dining with the Pharisee and had brought with her an alabaster jar of ointment. She waited behind him at his feet, weeping, and her tears

Luke 7:36–50 NJB

fell on his feet, and she wiped them away with her hair; then she covered his feet with kisses and anointed them with the ointment.

When the Pharisee who had invited him saw this, he said to himself, 'If this man were a prophet, he would know who this woman is and what sort of person it is who is touching him and what a bad name she has.' Then Jesus took him up and said, 'Simon, I have something to say to you.' He replied, 'Say on, Master.' 'There was once a creditor who had two men in his debt; one owed him five hundred denarii, the other fifty. They were unable to pay, so he let them both off. Which of them will love him more?' Simon answered, 'The one who was let off more, I suppose.' Jesus said, 'You are right.'

Then he turned to the woman and said to Simon, 'You see this woman? I came into your house, and you poured no water over my feet, but she has poured out her tears over my feet and wiped them away with her hair. You gave me no kiss, but she has been covering my feet with kisses ever since I came in. You did not anoint my head with oil, but she has anointed my feet with ointment. For this reason I tell you that her sins, many as they are, have been forgiven her, because she has shown such great love. It is someone who is forgiven little who shows little love.' Then he said to her, 'Your sins are forgiven.' Those who were with him at table began to say to themselves, 'Who is this man, that even forgives sins?' But he said to the woman, 'Your faith has saved you; go in peace.'

In his insightful book *The Friendship Factor* Alan Loy McGinnis says:

Jesus placed great value on relationships. He chose to spend much of his time deepening his connections with a few significant persons rather than addressing the crowds. What is more, his teaching was filled with practical suggestions on how to befriend people and how to relate to friends. The commandment on this topic was so important that he introduced it with an opening flag: 'A new commandment I give to you, that you love one another; even as I have loved you, that you also love one another. By this all men will know that you are my disciples, if you have love for one another' (John 13:34–35).

Alan Loy McGinnis has some encouraging things to say about our capacity for friendship. We don't need to be clever and we don't need to be extroverts:

You may or may not be the life of the party. If not, that will have little to do with your learning to love and be loved. In fact, as we will see later, you may be more capable of good relationships than the man who wears lampshades at the party and keeps them laughing all evening.

In my hometown an obscure nurseryman died recently. His name was Hubert Bales, and he was the shyest man I ever met. When he talked, he squirmed, blinked his eyes rapidly, and smiled nervously.

Hubert never ran in influential circles. He grew shrubs and trees, working with his hands the plot of land left him by his father. He was anything but an extrovert.

Yet when Hubert died, his funeral was the largest in the history of our little town. There were so many people that they filled even the balcony of the church.

Why did such a shy man win the hearts of so many people? Simply because, for all his shyness, Hubert knew how to make friends. He had mastered the principles of caring, and for more than sixty years he had put people first. Perhaps because they recognized that his generosity of spirit was an extra effort for someone so retiring, people loved him back. By the hundreds.

A friend is someone who likes you. Hubert liked people, and Jesus liked people. If we don't, we shan't be very good at reaching people. But even when we are really friends with someone we shall not agree about everything, and one thing we disagree about may be the gospel. Judas disagreed with Jesus, and Jesus 'failed' with Judas – even though right to the very end he reached out to him because he loved him. In his commentary on John's gospel William Barclay writes about the Last Supper:

It is the place of Judas that is of special interest. It is quite clear that Judas was in a position in which Jesus could speak to him privately without the others overhearing it. There is a kind of private conversation here going on between Jesus and Judas. Now if that be so there is only one place in which Judas could be sitting. He must have been sitting on Jesus' *left*, so that, just as John's head was in Jesus' breast, Jesus' head was in Judas' breast. And the revealing thing about that is that *the place on the left of the host was the place of highest honour, kept for the most intimate friend*. When that meal

57

began, Jesus must have said to Judas: 'Judas, come and sit beside me tonight; I want specially to talk to you. The very inviting of Judas to that seat was an appeal.

But there is more than that. For the host to offer the guest a special tit-bit, a special morsel from the dish, was again a sign of special friendship. When Boaz wished to show how much he honoured Ruth, he invited her to come and dip her morsel in the wine (Ruth 2:14). T. E. Lawrence told how when he sat with the Arabs in their tents, sometimes the Arab chief would tear a choice piece of fat mutton from the whole sheep which was before them and hand it to him, often a most embarrassing favour to a western palate, for it had to be eaten! So when Jesus handed the morsel to Judas, again it was a mark of special affection . . .

There is tragedy here. Again and again Jesus appealed to that dark heart, and again and again Judas remained unmoved. God save us from being thus completely impervious to the appeal of love.

William Barclay, The Gospel of John

If even the love of Christ couldn't win the heart of Judas then we have to recognize that some people can never be won. But everyone needs to be loved and everyone needs a friend, even if they don't recognize their own need. So our friendship and our love have to be like the love of God. Jesus told us so in the Sermon on the Mount:

**Matthew 5:43–48 NJB**

You have heard how it was said, You will love your neighbour and hate your enemy. But I say this to you, love your enemies and pray for those who persecute you; so that you may be children of your Father in heaven, for he causes his sun to rise on the bad as well as the good, and sends down rain to fall on the upright and the wicked alike. For if you love those who love you, what reward will you get? Do not even the tax collectors do as much? And if you save your greetings for your brothers, are you doing anything exceptional? Do not even the gentiles do as much? You must therefore set no bounds to your love, just as your heavenly Father sets none to his.

An old hymn puts it in old-fashioned words, but what it says is as up-to-date as this morning's sunrise and as vital as the air we breathe:

Out in the darkness,
Shadowed by sin,
Souls are in bondage,
Souls we would win;
How can we win them?
How show the way?
'Love never faileth',
Love is the way.

Think how the Master
Came from above,
Suffered on Calvary,
Breathing out love;
Think how He loves us,
E'en when we stray:
We must love others,
Love is His way.

See, they are waiting,
Looking at you,
Silently watching
All that you do;
Seeming so careless,
Hardened and lost:
'Love never faileth',
Count not the cost.

'Love never faileth',
Love is pure gold;
Love is what Jesus
Came to unfold;
Make us more loving,
Master, we pray,
Help us remember,
Love is Thy way.

F. Kirkland

The lovely thing about love is that it is nice to be with. It doesn't go round with a long face looking noble. It has a sense of humour and it sees the funny side of people. When someone loves us they can laugh at us and we don't mind. We know we are loved just as we are, but we also know that there are some areas of ourselves that aren't all they might be, and that love desires them to be all that they might be.

It is love that reaches out to people. First of all to love them just as they are because they are who they are – unique in all the world. But then love reaches out to people to communicate with them. To say the things to them that only love dares to say – and that they will only ever listen to when love says it. And love can say some tough things to its beloved:

When Christianity says that God loves man, it means that God *loves* man: not that He has some 'disinterested', because really indifferent, concern for our welfare, but that, in awful and surprising truth, we are the objects of His love. You asked for a loving God; you have one. The great spirit you so lightly invoked, the 'lord of terrible aspect', is present: not a senile benevolence that drowsily wishes you to be happy in your own way, not the cold philanthropy of a conscientious magistrate, nor the care of a host who feels responsible for the comfort of his guests, but the consuming fire Himself, the Love that made the worlds, persistent as the artist's love for his work and despotic as a man's love for a dog, provident and venerable as a father's love for a child, jealous, inexorable, exacting as love between the sexes. How this should be, I do not know: it passes reason to explain why any creatures, not to say creatures such as we, should have a value so prodigious in their Creator's eyes. It is certainly a burden of glory not only beyond our deserts but also, except in rare moments of grace, beyond our desiring . . .

C. S. Lewis, *The Problem of Pain*

Love reaches out to people all the time. God *is* love. A mnemonic to define the word 'grace' says that it is God Reaching After Creatures Everywhere. Before we can reach out to people for the right reasons we have to love them. And in terms of the church reaching out to people there are various ways of doing it and of deciding to whom we should be reaching out.

There are various things that can help us to identify people with a degree of openness to God. One thing is that anybody who is a good friend of an openly Christian person is showing a degree of openness to God. When C.S. Lewis was an unbeliever at Oxford he realized, to his bewilderment, that all his closest friends were Christians – and it was soon after that that he became a Christian himself.

People who are open to Christianity but not quite managing to believe yet, will come to church occasionally or take a parish magazine. They may want to be married in church. They will probably want their babies to be baptised, and they may send their children to Sunday school. All these things are signposts to point us in the direction of the right people. They are putting out signals that are saying to us, 'We're interested . . . we're wanting to make some sort of connection . . .' Then we have to ask ourselves, 'How can we engage with these people and help them to make the connection?'

There are three ways that we can try to do it, and different ways will be helpful to different people. So we shall probably have to use all three methods. First we can ask them to come to church, or to a mission. Second, we can meet somewhere in the middle – in our homes or in a pub or a hotel. Third, we can go to them in their own homes.

## WAYS IN WHICH THEY CAN COME TO US

In Gavin's experience there are two fundamental ways of working with the 'they come to us' strategy.

## The special service

First there is the traditional idea of a Special Service. An invitation service, or a service with a special theme, is a good idea, and in many places it will be very effective. But it will never work if all that we do is to put up a notice outside the church to tell any passers-by who happen to read it that 'Evangelist Hiram Bloggs will be preaching here next Sunday.' That is a recipe to empty the church rather than to fill it.

The planning and the preparation have to be done well in advance, and the invitations have to be personal. They ought to be printed, and they ought to be put into people's hands – not posted or even personally delivered through their letter box.

The most important thing in our planning and preparation is to start off with special prayer, and for people to go on praying.

The service and the publicity for it should be built round a theme. It is no use building it round a special speaker (even

though we may manage to get one) because people who don't go to church won't realize why he or she is special. The only evangelist who they have ever heard of is Billy Graham, and there are no other names that are going to pull them in. The saintly bishop with a shining face who speaks like an angel, and the Spring Harvest speaker who affected us so powerfully, will both produce equally blank expressions on people's faces when they see their names written in enormous letters on the invitation. 'Who's he?' they will ask.

But ask them, 'Can you make sense of Life?' (as the Mission 89 posters asked all over England and Wales), and you have made an instant connection that means something to them. They have probably been struggling to make sense of life for a long time, and now here is someone (whoever he or she is) who might be able to help them.

What we have to ask is: 'Who will come to this sort of service?' The people most likely to come to an occasion in church will probably have had some experience of church before. But it might have been a long time ago, and it was probably fairly traditional. So if we plan a service which is right up-to-date and rather way-out, with most of the hymns written in the last two years including the very latest one from Graham Kendrick, they are going to feel uncomfortable.

It is hard enough for them to be in an unfamiliar place. But it will be even harder if the hymns are unfamiliar as well. If they know them, then they will feel more at ease and they won't be irritated. We need to be sensitive to people's expectations. If we are not, we shall put their backs up and they will be resistant to the message we want them to hear. The message is there in the old hymns just as much as the new ones, and the reason why we are having this service is so that people will listen to the message – not so that we can have a sing-along of our new favourites. An essential part of an invitation service is that people should be able to sing some of the old favourites.

63

It is important that the service is not too long. If there is to be time for a decent presentation of the gospel, and perhaps some time for a simple invitation procedure, then the speaker should be in the pulpit not later than thirty-five and preferably thirty minutes after the start of the service. If it is an Anglican service that can be quite difficult to achieve, so there needs to be some careful planning on timing.

Probably there should only be one Bible reading – and it should be well read and rehearsed.

The prayers need to be thought about very carefully and planned in advance.

We must never pray *at* people. The sort of prayer that says, 'O Lord, we pray for those here tonight who do not know you,' is definitely not on! We should have been praying for them in the months before the service – and if we have not been doing so then the service is unlikely to be effective.

What the people at our special service will want to see and to hear, and what will make an impression, is that we are people who care about what is going on in the world.

Gavin tells a story about an executive whose firm had moved. Until he could find somewhere for his family to live he was in rooms in someone else's house. On his first Sunday there he noticed people walking past the house on their way to the local parish church, and he was astonished at how many there were. So, rather like Moses wanting to investigate the burning bush, he said to himself, 'I must turn aside and see this strange thing! Here is A Church with People Going In!' So he went in as well, and sat at the back.

What shook him right to the core was the meaningfulness of the worship and in particular the intercessions. He had stumbled upon a group of people who really cared about what was

going on in the world, and it captured his heart for God. Afterwards he said to the curate, 'By the time the man got into the pulpit I was ready to sign on any dotted line he put in front of me.'

If we want to know what to pray about then all we have to do is to read the newspapers. At the lunch-hour service which has been started in St Mary's, Reigate, the vicar, Richard Thomson, takes *The Times* into the pulpit and prays through the front page of it.

One Sunday morning Gavin and Mary went to church feeling deeply upset by the news that a hundred American soldiers had been killed by a car bomb in the Lebanon. The US Seventh Fleet was drawing into the Straits of Lebanon, and Moscow had issued a warning. But after the intercessions Gavin looked at Mary and was furious. He whispered in her ear, 'So I've got it all wrong. We haven't got another world problem on our hands! Nothing's happened in the Lebanon!'

To Gavin's fury, all that church was praying about were things like 'the quality of our fellowship . . .' and matters that came totally within the parish boundaries. It wasn't that they weren't suitable matters to pray about. They were. But we are also supposed to be praying about what is happening in the world — and if the world comes into our congregation and listens to prayers that relate to the world they will say, 'This is good. This is real life as *we* know it.' They will be aware that we are living in the real world and wrestling with the vast problems that the world has to face.

The title or the theme that we choose for the talk at the invitation service could be about the problems of the world. 'What is wrong with our world?' 'How to mend a broken world.' It could be a very matter-of-fact title, like 'Is Christ relevant to the 1990s', or 'Is Christianity true?' Gavin was once asked to speak on 'If you get to where you're going, where will you be?'

At the service itself it is particularly valuable for the preacher to draw his (or her) sermon to a conclusion with a prayer of commitment for those people for whom it is appropriate. Then the preacher could issue an invitation something along these lines:

'If you have prayed that prayer, or if you have prayed a prayer like it at some time recently, I would like you to come up and tell me. I have got a little leaflet that was particularly written for someone in your situation, and it will tell you some more about the Christian life and how to go into it more deeply.'

Then the speaker or the minister could say that 'There is something else we should like to suggest as well. In a month's time we shall be starting a group on "Christian basics". And you will really get the most out of this service if you will join that group. And when you come up, we will give you the details of that as well.'

St Helen's Church, Bishopsgate, in the City of London, uses its guest service as a recruiting service for its beginners' group. When Gavin preached at a guest service in that church there was an application form to join the beginners' group on every chair, and a letter box at the back of the church to put the form in. If someone wanted to join they simply wrote their name and address on the form and put it into the box on their way out. But Gavin suggested that if they had prayed the prayer of commitment that night and also wanted to join a beginners' group then they should come up and give the application form to him personally.

At a guest service it is helpful to serve coffee and coke at the back of the church afterwards. It is no good asking people to move to the hall. A lot of them will get lost on the way and go home instead.

It is helpful, too, to have a good book table or bookstall at the back of the church, with some church members near it who can be sensitive to the needs of the people browsing at it – and be ready to say, 'Yes, I think this book would be just right for you . . . but if you are really interested then you may find that our beginners' group is right up your street . . .'

Invitation services in church are an important part of mission. But we ought not to hold them too often. Back in the 1950s some churches used to hold a 'Guest Service' every month. But after about six months the congregation had worked the seam dry and run out of friends to invite. So it ended up being a 'Happy Hymn Sunday'. Probably we should have only two or three services of this sort every year. But have them we must, because they back up the more gentle and continuous evangelism of befriending.

I would spend my best efforts to make them follow him whose first servants were the fishermen of Galilee, for with all my heart I believe that that Man holds the secret of life, and that only the man who obeys him can ever come to know the God who is the root and crown of our being, and whom to know is freedom and bliss.

George Macdonald, *The Marquis of Lossie*

*Group material, meditation, and prayers for chapter 4:*
WAYS TO MAKE EVANGELISM HAPPEN

*A Prayer for the Decade of Evangelism*

Lord Jesus Christ, in your great love for the world, you came to die that we may live and called us to follow you, to carry the gospel to the lost, and to extend your Kingdom of righteousness in this world of pain and suffering and fear.

Give to us and your whole Church grace to hear your call and to obey your word; and set our hearts on fire with love for you and all humankind so that we may engage in bold and adventurous evangelism to turn many from darkness to light; and grant that, attempting great things for you, we may expect great things from you; who, with the Father and the Holy Spirit are one God, now and forever.   Amen
The Church of Southern Africa

1.  Read out Luke 7:36–50 slowly and suggest that people close their eyes and see what is happening in the story in their mind's eye.
2.  Ask everyone to reflect for a moment or two on the passage, and then let each one (if they are willing – if not, ask them to say 'Pass') say what especially came home to them.
3.  Read out the extract from *The Friendship Factor* (see pages 56–57). Then talk about friendship. Think about your own best friends, and consider what it is that makes them special for you. St Ailred of Rievaulx wrote on Christian fellowship: 'The reward of friendship is itself. The man who hopes for anything else does not understand what true friendship is.' Consider this in terms of this chapter.
4. Talk about the possibility of having a special invitation service in your church. Plan it, very roughly, and get one person to write down the plans. Think of two or three themes for it that would be of interest to your area. Then take the idea to your church council.

*Meditation*

Read out very slowly, with silences and spaces for reflection:

Shut your eyes and be quiet and relaxed . . . be still for a few moments in silence . . . They called Jesus a friend of publicans and sinners . . . think what it must have been like for them . . . but everyone needs a friend . . . famous people need them just as much as ordinary people . . . successful people in the world's eyes just as much as less successful people . . . everyone needs someone they can trust . . . someone who likes them . . . Remember the children's story by Joan Walsh Anglund . . . 'A friend is someone who likes you . . .'

Whom do you like? Whom do you like who isn't a Christian? . . . Think of just one such person . . . will you commit yourself to be their friend? . . . just for the sake of the friendship . . . Remember St Ailred of Rievaulx . . . 'The reward of friendship is itself. The man who hopes for anything else does not understand what true friendship is . . .' For two or three minutes, reflect on your own friendships . . . ask God to show you what they are like . . . to show you how good a friend you are . . . to show you how to be even better . . .

Lord Jesus Christ, you are the friend of publicans and sinners . . . and you said to your disciples, 'I no longer call you servants but friends . . .' May we know you as our friend . . . Show us the way of friendship . . . show us how to be friends . . . 'If you love those who love you, what reward will you get? . . . You must set no bounds to your love, just as your heavenly Father sets no bounds to his . . .'

Then ask people to pray their own prayers out loud, if they would like to.


## A Prayer for the Decade of Evangelism

O God, send your blessing upon us in this Decade of Evangelism. Prepare our hearts so that we may be open to the guidance and renewing influence of your Holy Spirit. Revive and sanctify your disciples in this place and show us, each one, what you would have us do. We ask this in the Name of Jesus who is the Way, the Truth and the Life.   Amen

The Church in Wales

70

# 5. More Ways to Make Evangelism Happen

'What?! Me a missionary!'

The answer to that question, if you are a Christian, is 'Yes'.

Archbishop Robert Runcie said right at the start of the Decade of Evangelism that 'evangelism is essentially the task of the local member churches. The officers in evangelism are the bishops and clergy, and the laity are the missionaries.'

The church as a whole, and every individual member of it, is called and sent into all the world to preach the gospel and to be the light of the world.

We all have to be lights that shine in the world to the glory of God the Father – 'You in your small corner, and I in mine', as the children's hymn has it – and if you don't shine, or I don't, then perhaps the place where we live or work will stay in

71

darkness – unless God sends another light to shine in it. But for the time being he has sent you and me, so we had better get on with the shining and the reaching out.

In his letter to the Christians in Philippi Paul tells them to look to the quality of their own lives so that they can offer the word of life to the world:

Philippians
2:12–16 GNB So then, dear friends, as you always obeyed me when I was with you, it is even more important that you obey me now while I am away from you. Keep on working with fear and trembling to complete your salvation, because God is always at work in you to make you willing and able to obey his own purpose.
Do everything without complaining or arguing, so that you may

be innocent and pure as God's perfect children, who live in a world of corrupt and sinful people. You must shine among them like stars lighting up the sky, as you offer them the message of life.


## More ways of reaching out

In the last chapter we looked at just one way of reaching out to people to offer them the message of life – the special invitation service in church. In this chapter we shall look at more ways of reaching out.


## The after-dinner speaker

Another way to get them to come to us is to invite them to dinner and have an after-dinner speaker. The speaker talks about the gospel, perhaps with a title such as 'Being a Christian in Business', or 'Being a Christian Psychologist' – and it is often better to have someone with a secular job than someone who works in the church.

The guests are told in advance that this is going to happen. It would be a disgraceful piece of sharp practice to invite them to dinner and *not* tell them, and horribly dishonouring to the Christ we say we follow – who is 'the way and the *truth* and the life'. If we don't tell people what is going to happen then we are not doing the truth. And don't say, 'But no one would *ever* do such a thing!' because I know people who *have* done it – and also the people whom they have done it to.

There are two ways to set up the dinner. It can be either a sit-down meal or a buffet, and whichever it is the meal has to be first-class and the decor elegant and inviting. Limp lettuce leaves, quartered tomatoes, and cold egg-yellow quiche won't put people in the right sort of mood to listen receptively to the speaker. Good food, good wine, soft lighting and flowers on

73

the table will. A relaxed, comfortable atmosphere is vital to this sort of occasion.

Some Christians are non-drinkers as a matter of principle – but they ought not to force their principles down other people's throats. We are trying to win them for Christ – not to get them to sign the pledge.

A supper with a speaker is an excellent format for young parents. A good approach for them is to choose a theme such as 'Our Children and God'. The speaker can then say something like the following: 'Most of us here tonight are parents, and all of us want the best for our children. We believe that God is important to them, although we don't necessarily understand quite how and what that means for us. So tonight we are going to look at the whole issue of how we can help our children to discover God . . .'

The logical line to follow in a talk like this is to say at some point: 'But we can't help them to discover God if we haven't discovered him for ourselves . . .'

There are other things the speaker can touch on, such as what we can learn from our children about God – which leads straight in to the teaching of Jesus:

At that time the disciples came to Jesus, saying, 'Who is the greatest in the kingdom of heaven?' And calling to him a child, he put him in the midst of them, and said, 'Truly, I say to you, unless you turn and become like children, you will never enter the kingdom of heaven. Whoever humbles himself like this child, he is the greatest in the kingdom of heaven.

'Whoever receives one such child in my name receives me; but whoever causes one of these little ones who believe in me to sin, it would be better for him to have a great millstone fastened round his neck and to be drowned in the depth of the sea.'

**Matthew 18:1–6 RSV**

At the end of the talk a helpful way to introduce the final prayers is to say, 'Now I am going to end with two short prayers – a prayer for our children, and a prayer for those of us who are parents . . .'

Sometimes, especially at slightly more formal occasions when people are sitting at tables, it can be useful to put a card and a ball-point pen by each plate. At some point in the talk the speaker will refer to it, and say, 'We shall tell you what it is all about a bit later on.' Then, at the end of the talk, the speaker can say:

'We are going to have coffee now – and while it is being served I would like to tell you what the card and the pen are for. What we would like you to do is to write down your reactions to what you have heard tonight. It will be a help for us when we plan future occasions like this. We don't want you to sign the card – just put it in the box that you will find by the door on your way out . . .

'But if you have prayed that prayer of commitment and you really are interested in taking things a bit further, then as well as writing down any comments you have, would you just add your name and address so that we can get in touch with you and let you have something to read.'

The advantage of doing it that way is that *everyone* is writing and so nobody feels conspicuous.

Even at a buffet supper it is important to hold the coffee back until the very end, because that will encourage people to stop on and talk to each other. It also gives an opportunity for the hosts to mill around and talk to the guests. If the coffee is served immediately after the meal then some people will get up and go immediately after the talk.

The 'meal with an after-dinner speaker' is a good format. It is the sort of occasion that quite a few people are used to, and they feel comfortable when they listen to a speaker and are given information. The ideal speaker will have a natural sense of humour which will show in the talk.

Gavin prefers a buffet supper to a sit-down dinner, although even at a buffet there will be small tables, and chairs to sit down. The disadvantage of a formal dinner is that everyone is anchored in the same place, between the same people, for the whole evening.

At a buffet people can change tables and go and sit with someone else. At the end the coffee should be served from a table or a serving hatch and people should be encouraged to come up and get their own. Then they can gravitate towards the people they feel most comfortable with.

It is a good idea to give out a notice about something which the church is about to set up – perhaps a beginners' course on Christianity. We need to be looking out all the time for the thing which will take people on to the next step.

It is also good to have a book table, with people standing near to it ready to chat – just as in the 'invitation to a special service in church' format.

If the supper evening has been for young parents then that is an ideal time to tell them about the Mothering Sunday service. We can even pick up the American idea and have a Father's Day service. Or tell them about the Christmas services, or the Easter services, or the Harvest Festival.

It is probably best to preach at all of those services in a way that strictly relates to the occasion and says what it is about. However enthusiastic an evangelist the preacher may be, the occasion should not be used as an excuse to do a great gospel beat-up. The gospel can be brought out and made quite explicit, but it will be more effective if no great pressure is put upon people to do something about it instantly.

However, a notice could be given out (along with the other notices) to say, 'We have a beginners' course starting in a month for people who would be interested, and you will find details in the pew in front of you.'

## The 'Census of Favourite Hymns'

Some churches run a census in the district on people's favourite hymns. They advertise the census in relation to a service which they are going to hold on 'Blackpool's Five Favourite Hymns' or 'Tolworth's Top Ten Hymns' (though that might go on a bit too long for most people).

A good time to have such a service can be on the evening of Harvest Festival, which can sometimes fall a bit flat. Perhaps the Salvation Army band can be brought in to play and to accompany the hymns, and the hymns themselves are made the basis of the talk. It is an opportunity for the preacher to explain

the message more deeply. This is a variation on the 'invitation service', but rather an unusual one.

## WAYS OF MEETING IN THE MIDDLE

### The 'Meal with a Meaning'

To have a 'Meal with a Meaning' in someone's home is one of several home-based events that we shall consider. Again, it is

essential never to deceive people. Invite them to a 'Meal with a Meaning' or a 'Dialogue Dinner' and tell them what the subject is going to be.

Perhaps it could be 'The Meaning of Christianity Today', or even 'Our Doubts about Christianity'. People like to air their doubts, and they do not often get a chance to discuss them with people who have faith. The paradoxical thing is that when they talk about their doubts they sometimes experience an upsurge of faith. Another subject could be 'Faith and Doubt'.

It is best to eat first (preferably buffet-style). And it is good to have a crowded room, because people feel less vulnerable. After the meal one or two can share their faith in Christ and then proceedings can be opened up for questions, comments, and even disagreements. The open discussion should not be too

long because the best exchanges often take place in twos and threes afterwards over a cup of coffee.

The 'Meal with a Meaning' is a middle-class way of reaching out and meeting in the middle. But there are other ways.

## 'Ale and Argument'

A very effective format for a 'one-off' event is to hire a room in the local pub, lay on some food, and let people buy whatever they want to drink. Everyone knows why they are there, and when they have all got some food on their plate and a glass in their hand someone starts off a discussion by asking a provocative question. Or it could start off with a speaker, and the arguments could go on all round the room after he has finished.

This way cuts across all our class barriers, because there are pubs all over the country – from the City of London to the inner city in Liverpool.

This format can also work on a more regular basis, with the room in the pub booked once a month on the same day and at the same time. People can know in advance what the subject is going to be, and it can be planned as a series. It is a good way to reach out to men, and there is something to be said for running some 'men only' events. Women seem to be better at talking, and men often talk more freely when women are not there.

Some readers may see that as a sexist comment, but it isn't. It is simply a description of the way things are. And we are in the business of reaching out to people as they are – not to people as they ought to be. Once they have heard the message of life and have accepted it, then men and women alike have within them the possibility of changing and growing into the person God means them to be.

## Other ways to have discussions

Some people are 'head-skilled' and other people are 'hand-skilled'. Those who are head-skilled are usually happy to socialize and talk to each other. Hand-skilled people may find it easier to meet in a more structured way that doesn't rely on clever talk.

What can work in this situation is for seven or eight people to meet every week in a house, and for a piece of paper to be handed out to everyone with a Bible passage on it (or else for everyone to be given the same edition of a gospel so that all the page numbers are the same). They should not be asked to read it out (a lot of perfectly intelligent people find reading difficult), but the leader should read it and then ask simple questions about what it says and what it means.

Another very good way to start a discussion with this or any group is to watch a video together and then talk about it.

Zefferelli's film *Jesus of Nazareth* is a superb one to use, but the leader has to do some work on it first and prepare some 'clips' for each discussion. There is enough material in it for several meetings.

Someone Gavin knows showed the whole of *Chariots of Fire* to his group and encouraged them to talk about it and discuss it all the way through, while it was still playing.

At events like these it is no use having a strict agenda which aims to get the group from point A to point B. The discussion has to be allowed to take its own course. We can encourage ourselves by remembering that the Holy Spirit is also present at the meeting, and delights to point people to Jesus.


## Ways to identify interested people

A very effective way to get in touch with people who have some interest in church and in Christianity is to put out cards and pens in the pews at all the Christmas services. When the notices are being given out the last notice should tell the people what the cards are for and at that point there should be a guided 'filling up the card' exercise. The notice will say something like:

'We would love to know the names and addresses of everyone who has worshipped with us at Christmas – so that when from time to time we are running some special event we can send you a note about it.'

Then invite everybody to fill in the cards, if they will, and say that in a moment the sidesmen will come to the end of the rows and collect them.

The same thing can be done again in the summer. In May or

June put out the cards for four consecutive weeks and say in the notices:

'If you consider yourself a member of this congregation we would like to put you on our congregational roll.'

The result of that exercise will be a valuable list of 'regulars' – and if we subtract that list from the Christmas list then we have identified our 'irregulars'.

The 'irregulars' form the fringe of the church, and they are the people amongst whom evangelism will happen most effectively. They have shown some interest, so our task is to reach out to them to try to deepend their interest.

## WAYS IN WHICH WE CAN GO TO THEM

This way of reaching out to people is probably the one that we shall find most difficult and find ourselves shrinking away from, because it involves visiting people in their homes.

A scheme was developed in America to train up church people to visit *where they are wanted.*

There are two sorts of church visiting. In the first we arrive unannounced on people's doorsteps, and say when we get there that we are from St Martha's Church. It is not a good idea to talk about God or the gospel unless they raise the subjects, and they probably won't. But this sort of visiting is a good way to get in touch with a lot of people and to discern where there might be further interest.

In the second sort of visiting we go to the people who have already shown some interest, and it is with them that the American scheme begins.

## Evangelism Explosion

In this scheme people are approached who have already been identified as having some interest in Christian things. They are asked, 'Would you be interested for two or three people from St Martha's to call on you and spend an evening discussing Christianity with you?' If they say 'No thank you!' that is the end of the story. If they say 'Yes' then a time is fixed to suit their convenience and three people go along.

We may think that three people is too many, but the number has been carefully thought out. The first reason is that it can be quite frightening for one person to go on their own. Second, if two people go it is good to have one of each sex, and if they are not husband and wife that might be misconstrued. Thirdly, it is a method of training. One person is the 'leader' and trained up to a point, and the other two go as less experienced people to learn how to do it. One day they will be the 'leader' with two apprentices.

Three people help to create a nice little roomful of people. It also means that, if everything goes well, then the person or the couple visited will already know three people from the local congregation and feel comfortable with them.

This Evangelism Explosion scheme is often parodied by people who don't know how it works, because of its two famous questions, which are meant to get people engaged in an evangelistic conversation. It may not be necessary to use them, because people may be quite happy to get into such a conversation without them. But they are specifically designed for people who are beating about the bush. When some British people hear what they are they cringe!

*First Question*: 'Have you come to a place in your spiritual life where you know for certain that if you were to die today you would go to heaven?'

Gavin often asks that question, but he puts it a rather more delicate and British way:

'Can I ask you a question?' he says. 'If (and God forbid) you were to walk under a bus tonight, have you come to a point in the way that you understand things that you know you would be safe with God?'

The point of asking a question like that is that it will evoke one of three answers. Either 'Yes', 'No', or 'I hope so'.

If the answer is 'No', then the questioner says, 'Then would you like me to tell you why I can say "Yes"?' If they say 'No' to that, then you have to abandon the whole subject. But if they say 'Yes', then you 'give them your testimony'.

But if the answer to the first question was 'Yes' or 'I hope so', then you ask them the

*Second Question*: 'Suppose you were to die tonight and stand before God, and he were to say to you, "Why should I let you into my heaven?", what would you say?'

It is quite important to have a twinkle in your eye and not to look too earnest when you ask such a question, but the answer will make it fairly clear whether a person is really trusting in Christ. If they say that God should let them in because they looked after their old mother for thirty years then it is clear that they are trusting in their own 'good works' rather than in the love and forgiveness of God-in-Christ.

In areas where people are blunt, and don't beat about the bush or mess around with words, Evangelism Explosion can be a remarkably effective approach. Their method is used *only when people know you are coming*, and the great thing about it is that it has an organization on the ground that can train you to start this scheme in your church.

85

There is a variation on Evangelism Explosion which was developed in a parish in the Midlands. It has the same basic dynamic, that it tries to find opportunities for three people to go to see a couple or a single person where they live. The three consist of one leader and two who are learning, and it is always set up in advance and the people know they are coming.

The difference is in the way you present it. You say to likely candidates, 'We have a little course in our church called "Understanding Christianity", and because people live the sort of lives they do you don't have to come to us. We'd like to bring the course to you, to your door. It takes six weeks and you can have six sessions – and you can stop the sessions any time you want to.' If they say 'Yes please', then the three people go along at the time that has been agreed, and because there are three plus one or two, that makes a nice group for discussion.

The course is based on looking at six sections of St Luke's gospel in the Good News Bible. Everyone is given a copy of the gospel, and they simply answer various questions. It was devised by Prebendary Michael Wooderson when he was in Aldridge, near Walsall, and he took it on to his next parish and it was equally effective there. Now there are people doing it all over the country. It has been published as a Grove booklet, *Good News Down the Street* which explains the course and sets out all the questions.

The likely candidates for such a course are perhaps a couple who want to have their baby baptised, or a couple enquiring about a wedding, or perhaps someone with a problem, or people who come to a family service, or perhaps people who are close friends of Christians in the church – and in that case the invitation to the course would come from the friends.

One great strength of this course rests in something which might seem to be rather a weakness and a deterrent – that it lasts for six weeks. But just because of the length of it you can go at whatever pace people want. In some weeks all the questions will not get answered, but they will have served their purpose, which is to get people talking themselves about Christ rather than simply listening to someone else talk and then either asking questions or being asked them.

This way of visiting and talking to one another can be a journey of discovery. If people stay with it, then by the end of six weeks they have made friends with the three people who have been coming to their home every week.

The great advantage which this method has over any other visitation evangelism is that a tremendously high percentage of those who come through the scheme actually become incorporated into the church. First of all they are linked to it indirectly through the three people they know, and then those people link them directly to the church and bring them right into it.

Another advantage of a six-week course is that it does not pressurize people to make a decision on the spot. Instead it encourages them to think about things over a longer period.

Finally, it encourages the whole process of pilgrimage, which is how most people become Christians.


## On Mission . . .

The members of the Church are impelled to engage in this activity because of the charity with which they love God and by which they desire to share with all men in the spiritual goods of this life and the life to come.

Vatican Council II

*Group material, meditation and prayers for chapter 5:*
MORE WAYS TO MAKE EVANGELISM HAPPEN

*A Prayer for the Decade of Evangelism*

Forgetting what lies behind and pressing on to the year 2000, come what may, we are resolved to reach every corner of our nation with the gospel of our Lord Jesus Christ.

You who are full of strength, call your people and put in their hearts zeal for evangelism. Enable us as a church to train and equip those you have called. Clothe them with your Spirit, empower us to proclaim Jesus King of all Kings.

The blood of the martyrs cannot allow us to rest when many of our brothers and sisters know no salvation.

O God, you are our hiding place. Go before us and soften the hearts of all these thy children whom the evil one has enslaved.

We put all our yearnings and cries before you with full assurance that you will not throw us out. But that you rejoice greatly when we fall on our knees and present our requests which you are ever ready to grant, through Jesus Christ our Lord and Redeemer.   Amen

The Church of Uganda

1. Read out Philippians 2:12–16 slowly and prayerfully, and suggest that people should shut their eyes as you read.
2. Ask each person to share with the rest what especially went home to their hearts as you read that passage from Philippians.
3. Talk briefly about 'Evangelism Explosion' and 'Good News Down the Street'. Would either of those ways of evangelism be suitable in your area? If you think they would, then plan to discuss them more deeply at the next meeting of this group.
4. The following exercise should run over this meeting and the next, final meeting. People can be thinking about the preliminary plans they have made today and polishing them up ready for next time. Divide into groups of two or three.

Let each group plan one or two of the following: A dinner with an after-dinner speaker, or a buffet supper with a speaker; a 'meal with a meaning'; a meeting in a pub (either a one-off meeting or a regular meeting); a video evening with discussion; an exercise in church to get the names and addresses of 'regulars' and 'irregulars'; a 'Census of Favourite Hymns' and its follow-up; plus any of your original ideas for the place where you live.

Make brief notes of your ideas and plans at this meeting, and at the next one write out the plans for each event on a sheet of A4 paper. That will be your working paper for the various ways of doing evangelism in your area.

### Meditation

Read out Philippians 2:12–16 again, perhaps even more slowly than at the beginning – and after the last sentence, 'You must shine among them like stars lighting up the sky, as you offer them the message of life', have a silence that lasts up to three or four minutes.

Ask people to pray their own prayers out loud, if they would like to.

Then, perhaps, sing the song 'Shine, Jesus, Shine' – or if you prefer not to sing, read out the words as a prayer.

### A Prayer for the Decade of Evangelism

> O God of life, do not let your light be darkened;
> O God of life, let your joy be known to us;
> O God of life, do not withhold your mercy from us;
> O God of life, crown us with your gladness.
> Deliver us from the troubles of the past
> and make us more faithful witnesses to your love
> made known in Jesus Christ our Lord.   Amen
>                          The Church in Wales

# 6. How Do People Become Christians?

When we ask 'How do people become Christians?' the only totally satisfactory answer is, 'God knows!'

The mystery of how a human being with a human nature becomes a sharer of the divine nature, one of the sons and daughters of the living God, is something we can only marvel at.

St Paul says that just as the light shone in the darkness at the creation of the world, so it shines in the darkness of the human heart to create a new, eternal life:

**2 Corinthians 4:6 NIV** For God, who said, 'Let light shine out of darkness,' made his light shine in our hearts to give us the light of the knowledge of the glory of God in the face of Christ.

90

We see the result of the shining in the new life of the new creation, but we do not know how it came into being any more than Job knew how the creation of the earth took place. God speaks to him from the heart of the tempest and questions him:

Where were you when I laid the foundation of the earth? Job 38:4–12, 19–21 RSV
   Tell me, if you have understanding.
Who determined its measurements – surely you know!
   Or who stretched the line upon it?
On what were its bases sunk,
   or who laid its cornerstone,
when the morning stars sang together,
   and all the sons of God shouted for joy?

Or who shut in the sea with doors
   when it burst forth from the womb;
when I made clouds its garment,
   and thick darkness its swaddling band,
and prescribed bounds for it,
   and set bars and doors,
and said, 'Thus far shall you come, and no farther,
   and here shall your proud waves be stayed'?

Have you commanded the morning since your days began,
   and caused the dawn to know its place? . . .

Where is the way to the dwelling of light,
   and where is the place of darkness,
that you may take it to its territory
   and that you may discern the paths to its home?
You know, for you were born then,
   and the number of your days is great!

At the end of God's questioning Job is so stunned by the glory that he has seen in created things that he stops questioning their Creator:

Job 42:3 RSV

> I have uttered what I did not understand,
> things too wonderful for me,
> which I did not know.

This may seem a strange place to start a chapter on 'How Do People Become Christians?' But we need to start with the mystery and not with our own very limited knowledge. And when we are talking to other people about the mystery we need to be sensitive.

We know that the New Testament uses the image of the new birth, but sometimes we use the imagery with all the tenderness of a battering ram.

A very hard-line Christian once told me proudly of his encounter with the local MP's wife when she was electioneering on behalf of her husband. 'Will you be voting Conservative?' she asked him — and whether he said yes or no isn't the point of the story and I can't remember. The point is what he subsequently said to her:

'Now can I ask you a question?'

'Yes, of course,' she replied. So he asked it.

'Will you tell me whether you have been born again?'

She didn't give him an answer, but he worked it out for himself. His voice was triumphant as he told me his conclusion:

'She obviously wasn't – because she simply didn't know what I was talking about!'

That is an example of how people *don't* become Christians. Here is an example of how they do – an account in John's gospel of the mysterious way in which a man draws close to the kingdom of heaven in an encounter with Christ the King. Every such encounter is unique, but however it happens it is always there in the heart of the mystery of the new creation.

Now there was a man of the Pharisees, named Nicodemus, a ruler of the Jews. This man came to Jesus by night and said to him, 'Rabbi, we know that you are a teacher come from God; for no one can do these signs that you do, unless God is with him.' John 3:1–17 RSV
Jesus answered him, 'Truly, truly, I say to you, unless one is born anew, he cannot see the kingdom of God.'
Nicodemus said to him, 'How can a man be born when he is old? Can he enter a second time into his mother's womb and be born?'
Jesus answered, 'Truly, truly, I say to you, unless one is born of water and the Spirit, he cannot enter the kingdom of God. That which is born of the flesh is flesh, and that which is born of the Spirit is spirit. Do not marvel that I said to you, "You must be born anew." The wind blows where it wills, and you hear the sound of it, but you do not know whence it comes or whither it goes; so it is with every one who is born of the Spirit.'
Nicodemus said to him, 'How can this be?'
Jesus answered him, 'Are you a teacher of Israel, and yet you do not understand this? Truly, truly, I say to you, we speak of what we know, and bear witness to what we have seen; but you do not receive our testimony. If I have told you earthly things and you do not believe, how can you believe if I tell you heavenly things? No one has ascended into heaven but he who descended from heaven, the Son of man. And as Moses lifted up the serpent in the wilderness, so must the Son of man be lifted up, that whoever believes in him may have eternal life.'
For God so loved the world that he gave his only Son, that whoever

believes in him should not perish but have eternal life. For God sent the Son into the world, not to condemn the world, but that the world might be saved through him.

Some sections of the church would say that people are only converted when they 'hear the true preaching of the evangel'. But the truth of the matter is that people are converted because the wind blows where it wills. They turn (which is what the word 'convert' means) and begin to put their allegiance in Christ through encountering Christ in other people, or perhaps in their own private search – and all because the wind of the Spirit is blowing.

But the gospel does have to be preached, and the Spirit uses what Christians do and say to bring other people to a saving knowledge of Christ.

Adrian Plass has written a book called *A Smile on the Face of God; The Unusual Story of Philip Ilott*. It is a true, profoundly moving story, and once I started to read it I couldn't put it down.

Philip has suffered all his life, starting with a long history of sexual abuse as a small child. He is a priest, and his life demonstrates how the expression of Christian faith can have quite different roots.

The description of the book on the cover says that 'His high churchmanship has social and emotional origins: many of his experiences and joys belong in the evangelical and charismatic wing of the church, while other practices are related much more to the devotional and sacramental traditions. Could it be that God is by no means putting all his eggs in one denominational basket?'

Philip contracts multiple sclerosis and his life is restricted to a wheel chair. But he has an amazing gift of counselling, and his compassion and perceptive insights are being used more and more. The story closes with a remarkable development: a real-life unexpected ending which takes place after the book has been written.

Early on in the book it tells how Philip becomes a Christian. That happens because the wind of the Spirit wills to blow within his heart — but human beings are also involved in the process. One of them is Sandy, a tough, red-haired little Scotsman, with whom Philip and four or five other servicemen share a room in the army.

Sandy is a Christian in a personal, deeply committed way, and Philip watches him suffering night after night in the barrack room when he kneels down by his bed to say his prayers. The moment he gets down on his knees the other soldiers bombard him with boots and belts and jokes. But Sandy never retaliates. He just goes on kneeling there — and Philip goes on watching.

Philip has already known something of God. When he had

worshipped in the cathedral church where he was a choirboy, and at his confirmation, he had been aware of something – or someone. But he knows that Sandy has something more, and he wants it for himself.

So he goes with Sandy to some Bible classes, and then they go to a Christian leadership weekend in the village of Ostenwalde. It is in a large country house, and for the first time in months Philip has a room to himself. From the moment he sees the speaker, Geoffrey Groebecker, he is deeply impressed. There is a quality of peace and stillness about him that he has never seen before.

As Geoffrey Groebecker gets up to speak there is a hush. 'This weekend,' he says, 'is going to introduce you to Jesus as a real person . . .' Philip is hooked. That is what he wants more than anything in the whole world. He listens intently to the rest of the talk, and on the next evening there is a film that shows the wonder and beauty and precision of the world that God has created. As the film ends Geoffrey Groebecker stands up, and it never occurs to Philip to doubt the next words he says:

'The God, who created the universe, and his son Jesus, can be as real to you as you want them to be . . . I'd like you to go back to your own rooms and speak to Jesus in your own words. Make him as real and personal for you as you possibly can . . .'

Philip makes his way back to his room, collects a cup of cocoa on the way, and gets himself ready for bed. Then he kneels down and tries to find an appropriate passage to read out of the Bible. But it is no good.

He was so strung up with anticipation that the words ran into each other and became meaningless. Tonight was a night for meeting the writer, not for reading the book. Laying his Bible aside on the bed, he closed his eyes, took a deep breath, and spoke like a hopeful child.

'Jesus, I saw in that film tonight the wonderful things you've done in creation, and I've seen so much of you in people like Sandy and especially in Geoffrey Groebecker. Now he's asked us to come back to our rooms and talk to you so that you become real to us. Would you please be real to me?'

There was a pause. Philip didn't know what he was waiting for, but the response, when it came, was more than anything he could ever have imagined.

It was as though a vast container of peace, happiness and sheer presence was upturned above his head, showering and drenching him with a sensation that was completely new. He felt that he was truly falling in love for the first time, as his spirit opened like a flower to receive a rain of joyful acknowledgement.

This love seemed to go deeper and further than any he had known previously: further than his feelings for parents or friends or Nellie from the Tenements; further than the secret friendship he had known and still knew with Alban; further and deeper even than the love he felt for his grandmother. Jesus was there – holding, cuddling, supporting, reaching down into him to comfort the little boy who had wanted so much to be loved and wanted by his mammy.

It felt like starting all over again, but with someone who wanted you – all of you, including the messy parts – right from the beginning.

It was almost like being born again . . .

The soldier called Sandy and the soldier called Geoffrey Groebecker both let their lights shine before the man called Philip – and because they did, he ended up glorifying God. But the wind of the Spirit had been blowing through his life for a long time.

So what about us? We may not be a Sandy or a Geoffrey Groebecker. We may not think our light is bright enough to show anyone the way. But we needn't get depressed. God has created each one of us differently, so that in different ways we can live to the praise of his glory and let the light shine.

What God is calling us to do is to be faithful to what we know and to tell other people what we know. He is calling them to himself, and it is God who will make them into the children of God, not us. But if we listen to the voice of God he will guide us to the right people, and we shall have the wisdom to say the right things. We shall meet the person whom God wants us to talk to as we go about the ordinary business of our everyday lives. Just as Jesus did.

John 4:4–42
NIV

Now he had to go through Samaria. So he came to a town in Samaria called Sychar, near the plot of ground Jacob had given to his son Joseph. Jacob's well was there, and Jesus, tired as he was from the journey, sat down by the well. It was about the sixth hour.

When a Samaritan woman came to draw water, Jesus said to her, 'Will you give me a drink?' (His disciples had gone into the town to buy food.)

The Samaritan woman said to him, 'You are a Jew and I am a Samaritan woman. How can you ask me for a drink?' (For Jews do not associate with Samaritans.)

Jesus answered her, 'If you knew the gift of God and who it is that asks you for a drink, you would have asked him and he would have given you living water.'

'Sir,' the woman said, 'you have nothing to draw with and the well is deep. Where can you get this living water? Are you greater than our father Jacob, who gave us the well and drank from it himself, as did also his sons and his flocks and herds?'

Jesus answered, 'Everyone who drinks this water will be thirsty again, but whoever drinks the water I give him will never thirst. Indeed, the water I give him will become in him a spring of water welling up to eternal life.'

The woman said to him, 'Sir, give me this water so that I won't get thirsty and have to keep coming here to draw water.'

He told her, 'Go, call your husband and come back.'

'I have no husband,' she replied.

Jesus said to her, 'You are right when you say you have no husband. The fact is, you have had five husbands, and the man you now have is not your husband. What you have just said is quite true.'

'Sir,' the woman said, 'I can see that you are a prophet. Our fathers worshipped on this mountain, but you Jews claim that the place where we must worship is in Jerusalem.'

Jesus declared, 'Believe me, woman, a time is coming when you will worship the Father neither on this mountain nor in Jerusalem. You Samaritans worship what you do not know; we worship what we do know, for salvation is from the Jews. Yet a time is coming and has now come when the true worshippers will worship the Father in spirit and truth, for they are the kind of worshippers the Father seeks. God is spirit, and his worshippers must worship in spirit and in truth.'

The woman said, 'I know that Messiah' (called Christ) 'is coming. When he comes, he will explain everything to us.'

Then Jesus declared, 'I who speak to you am he.'

Just then his disciples returned and were surprised to find him talking with a woman. But no one asked 'What do you want?' or 'Why are you talking with her?'

Then, leaving her water jar, the woman went back to the town and said to the people, 'Come, see a man who told me everything I ever did. Could this be the Christ?' They came out of the town and made their way towards him.

Meanwhile his disciples urged him, 'Rabbi, eat something.'

But he said to them, 'I have food to eat that you know nothing about.'

Then his disciples said to each other, 'Could someone have brought him food?'

'My food,' said Jesus, is to do the will of him who sent me and to finish his work. Do you not say, "Four months more and then the harvest"? I tell you, open your eyes and look at the fields! They are ripe for harvest. Even now the reaper draws his wages, even now he harvests the crop for eternal life, so that the sower and the reaper may be glad together. Thus the saying "One sows and another reaps" is true. I sent you to reap what you have not worked for. Others have done the hard work, and you have reaped the benefits of their labour.'

Many of the Samaritans from that town believed in him because of the woman's testimony, 'He told me everything I ever did.' So when the Samaritans came to him, they urged him to stay with them, and he stayed two days. And because of his words many more became believers.

They said to the woman, 'We no longer believe just because of what you said; now we have heard for ourselves, and we know that this man really is the Saviour of the world.'

How do people become Christians? That is the question we are looking at in this final chapter – and the answer seems to be that in one way or another they meet Christ and believe in him. The wind of the Spirit has been blowing in their hearts, and the light of the new creation has started to shine. But Christians are fellow-workers with God in the ministry of reconciliation, and they do the work for the love of God:

2 Corinthians
5:14—6:2 NJB

For the love of Christ overwhelms us when we consider that if one man died for all, then all have died; his purpose in dying for all humanity was that those who live should live not any more for themselves, but for him who died and was raised to life.

From now onwards, then, we will not consider anyone by human standards: even if we were once familiar with Christ according to human standards, we do not know him in that way any longer. So for anyone who is in Christ, there is a new creation: the old order is gone and a new being is there to see. It is all God's work; he reconciled us to himself through Christ and he gave us the ministry of reconciliation. I mean, God was in Christ reconciling the world to himself, not holding anyone's faults against them, but entrusting to us the message of reconciliation.

So we are ambassadors of Christ; it is as though God were urging you through us, and in the name of Christ we appeal to you to be reconciled to God. For our sake he made the sinless one a victim for sin, so that in him we might become the uprightness of God.

As his fellow-workers, we urge you not to let your acceptance of his grace come to nothing. As he said, 'At the time of my favour I have answered you; on the day of salvation I have helped you'; well, now is the real time of favour, now the day of salvation is here.

St Paul was a fellow-worker with God and an ambassador for Christ. He shared in God's work by the life that he lived and the preaching that he did. For Geoffrey Groebecker it was the same. The compelling power of a holy life, and then the words that he spoke at a meeting of soldiers. Sandy didn't say very much. He didn't speak at public meetings, but to Philip Ilott his whole life spoke about Christ.

All of us who are Christians are fellow-workers with God and ambassadors for Christ – and we are all involved in God's great work of saving the world that he loves. We aren't all called to be preachers, like St Paul or like Geoffrey Groebecker. But we are all called to be witnesses, like Sandy and like the woman at the well of Samaria, and to be lights that shine.

I am the light of the world . . .

John 8:12 RSV

You are the light of the world . . .

Matthew 5:14 RSV

Lord, the light of Your love is shining,
In the midst of the darkness, shining;
Jesus, Light of the World, shine upon us,
Set us free by the truth You now bring us,
Shine on me, shine on me.

Shine, Jesus, shine,
Fill this land with the Father's glory;
Blaze, Spirit, blaze, set our hearts on fire.
Flow, river flow, flood the nations with grace and mercy;
Send forth Your word, Lord,
and let there be light.

Graham Kendrick

## Group material, meditation and prayers for chapter 6:
### HOW DO PEOPLE BECOME CHRISTIANS?
### A Prayer for the Decade of Evangelism

Eternal and ever-loving Creator God, who desires not the death of sinners but rather delights that they may return to live with you, we ask you to look lovingly upon all your people, and especially give to those who have had no chance to know you the heart to pay reverence to you, and increase the faith, the hope, and the love within them. Send your Holy Spirit to your Church at this Decade of Evangelism, especially on us who pray and serve your call, that we may be used as the instruments of your peace, the witnesses and the proclaimers to share the good news of your Son Jesus Christ. And, with all whom you love, give us the joy to enter into your eternal

Kingdom, through the blessings of the Saviour, Jesus Christ our Lord. Amen

The Holy Catholic Church in Japan

1. Ask people to listen prayerfully as you read out the passage from Job at the start of this chapter – but first read out the verse from 2 Corinthians:

For God, who said, 'Let light shine out of darkness,' made his light shine in our hearts to give us the light of the knowledge of the glory of God in the face of Christ.

2. Continue working on the plans that you started to draw up last week (see page 89). Ask one (very reliable!) person (you don't want to lose them!) to take all the plans home and get them typed out and copied. Distribute them to your church council and to some people in the rest of the parish.

*Final Meditation*

Ask people to sit comfortably and to shut their eyes. Ask them to be aware of their breathing . . . and to remember that the Holy Spirit is the breath of God. Then, quite slowly, with spaces for silence and reflection, read out 2 Corinthians 5:14–6:2.

Finish the meditation with a three- or four-minute silence. Then ask people to repeat each phrase of the following prayer after you. It is a prayer for the Decade of Evangelism from the Church in Wales, based on some words by David Adam.

> I give my hands to you, Lord . . .
> I offer the work I do, Lord . . .
> I give my thoughts to you, Lord . . .
> I give my plans to you, Lord . . .
> I give my words to you, Lord . . .
> Give your hands to me, Lord . . .
> Let me have your joy, Lord . . .

Set me free to love, Lord . . .
Lead me in your truth, Lord . . .
Give your words to me, Lord . . .
Keep me close to you, Lord . . .

Amen

Then ask people to pray their own prayers out loud, if they would like to.

## A Prayer for the Decade of Evangelism

Lord, open to us the sea of your mercy
and water us with full streams from the riches of your grace and springs of your kindness.
Make us children of your peace,
kindle in us the fire of your love,
show in us the fear and love of your name,
strengthen our weakness,
and bind us close to you and to each other as we share in your mission to the world:
to your glory, Father, Son and Holy Spirit.   Amen

The Church in Wales

Finish by singing or reading aloud 'Shine, Jesus, Shine'.

# Sources of Quoted Material

INTRODUCTION

The song 'Shine, Jesus, Shine' by Graham Kendrick is copyright © 1988 Make Way Music, published by Kingsway Publications, and is used by permission of the publishers.

CHAPTER 1

Derek Worlock and David Sheppard, *With Christ in the Wilderness: Following Lent Together*, Bible Reading Fellowship 1989.
The Collect for Epiphany, *The Alternative Service Book 1980*, Copyright © The Central Board of Finance of the Church of England 1980, and used with permission.

CHAPTER 2

Catherine Marshall, *Mr Jones, Meet the Master*, Fontana 1964.
William Temple, *Christian Faith and Life*, SCM Press 1963.
George Appleton, *Journey for a Soul*, Collins 1976.

CHAPTER 3

Gavin Reid, *To Reach a Nation*, Falcon/Kingsway 1979.
Metropolitan Anthony, *God and Man*, Darton, Longman and Todd 1971. Used by permission of the publishers.

CHAPTER 4

Joan Walsh Anglund, *A Friend is Someone Who Likes You*, Collins 1959.

Alan Loy McGinnis, *The Friendship Factor*, Hodder and Stoughton 1979. Used by permission of the publishers.

William Barclay, Daily Study Bible, *The Gospel of John*, Saint Andrew Press 1955, vol. 2, p. 169. Used by permission of the publishers.

C. S. Lewis, *The Problem of Pain*, Fontana 1957, p. 35.

George MacDonald, *The Marquis of Lossie*, Everett & Co. Ltd 1912, p. 269.


CHAPTER 5

Michael Wooderson, *Good News Down the Street*, Grove Books 1990

Vatican Council II, *The Conciliar and Post Conciliar Documents*, 1981 edition, Fowler-Wright Books Ltd.


CHAPTER 6

Adrian Plass, *A Smile on the Face of God: The Unusual Story of Philip Ilott*, Hodder and Stoughton 1990. Used by permission of the publishers.

The song 'Shine, Jesus, Shine' by Graham Kendrick in Copyright © 1988 Make Way Music, published by Kingsway Publications and in use by permission of the publishers.

The prayer 'I give my hands . . .' is based on a prayer in David Adam, *The Edge of Glory*, Triangle Books 1985.

The prayers for the Decade of Evangelism used throughout this book are taken from material distributed by the Anglican Consultative Council.

# THANK GOD FOR THAT!
## by Tim Mayfield and James Jones
## with illustrations by Taffy

In response to many requests . . . an adult equivalent of *Following Jesus* (written by James Jones).

For enquirers and adults considering church membership, here are 31 readings which provide practical steps towards Christian faith. Each short section considers a different aspect of what it means to commit oneself to God, and contains a Bible passage (printed out in full), thoughtful comments and a prayer.

Based on an effective scheme of parish evangelism and training, *Thank God For That* will be welcomed by parishes and church centres, house groups and individuals.

Tim Mayfield is director of evangelism in a Halifax parish. James Jones is Vicar of Emmanuel, South Croydon; now well-known as an author and broadcaster, he specialized in family services when at Christ Church, Clifton. His books include a series of three for BRF aimed at young people *(Following Jesus; Serving Jesus; Praying With Jesus)*. Taffy's work is familiar from cartoon, filmstrip and video.

**'I am very happy to endorse the book, for I find it a most useful resource which could be given to people finding their way into faith.'**

*Canon John Finney*
*(Officer for the Decade of Evangelism)*

# WITH CHRIST IN THE WILDERNESS

## Following Lent together

## Derek Worlock and David Sheppard

In *With Christ In The Wilderness* the authors point to the Christian way of life for people today, especially those in our cities, through Bible passages, comment, prayers and true stories about people. The 48 daily readings are taken from the scripture readings used each day at the Eucharist during Lent.

Derek Worlock, Roman Catholic Archbishop of Liverpool, worked at Westminster and in Portsmouth before moving to Liverpool in 1976; he wrote, with David Sheppard, the best-selling *Better Together*.

David Sheppard, Bishop of Liverpool, is the Church of England's best-known cricketer; he worked in deprived parts of London before going to Liverpool in 1975; co-author of *Better Together*, he also wrote *Bias To The Poor* and *Built As A City*.

BRF books and their prices are obtainable at Christian bookshops or direct from the BRF, Ground Floor, Warwick House, 25 Buckingham Palace Road, London, SW1W 0PP. (A minimum of 75p will be charged for postage and packing.)

The Bible Reading Fellowship was founded 'to encourage the systematic and intelligent reading of the Bible, to emphasize its spiritual message and to take advantage of new light shed on Holy Scripture'.

Over the years the Fellowship has proved a trustworthy guide for those who want an open, informed and contemporary approach to the Bible. It retains a sense of the unique authority of Scripture as a prime means by which God communicates.

As an ecumenical organization, the Fellowship embraces all Christian traditions and its readers are to be found in most parts of the world.

# READING MARK IN GROUPS
## Frances Garland

Intended to facilitate informed and applied study of Mark's gospel by small groups. 'Friendly and comfortable', with no jargon. *Reading Mark in Groups* makes intelligent use of the best New Testament scholarship, in a form groups will understand and appreciate. The book is designed to enable anyone in the group to lead (no special leadership or theological skills are required) and offers practical suggestions on how to use the studies and how to lead the group.

18 studies cover the whole gospel (the author suggests how the course may be shortened to 12 or 9 studies); also included here are an index, maps, detailed diagrams and useful background notes on the text. Each study comprises a number of questions which focus the reader's attention on the key issues of the text, and a section called 'Facing the challenge' which considers how to apply them.

'Many books are published about the Bible: few encourage you to read it for yourself. But that is what Frances Garland has produced . . . All in all an excellent treatment.'

*Michael Green, Church Times*